"You have to be a romantic to invest yourself, your money,

and your time in cheese."

Anthony Bourdain

100. Prästost

Sweden | Semi-Soft | Cow

Prästost is a traditional cheddar-style cheese originating from Sweden. The name "Prästost" means "Priest Cheese," referring to its historical production in churches from the 16th to the 19th centuries, where it was used as a form of payment instead of money. Today, Prästost is primarily produced in factories, maintaining its distinctive character and rich heritage.

Prästost has a creamy, semi-soft texture. The cheese boasts intense and rich aromas, while the flavors are strong, salty, and spicy. Due to its robust flavors, Prästost is often enjoyed as a snack or incorporated into soups, adding depth and complexity to dishes. There are also special versions of this cheese cured in whiskey, known as Saaland Pfarr cheese, or Absolut vodka, referred to as VODCheese, offering unique twists on the traditional flavor profile.

The history of Prästost is deeply rooted in Swedish culture. Originally made by church congregations, the cheese played a significant role in the local economy, serving as a valuable commodity in a time when currency was scarce. This tradition continued for centuries, making Prästost an integral part of Swedish culinary history.

For a delightful wine pairing, consider a full-bodied red wine like a Cabernet Sauvignon. The wine's bold tannins and dark fruit flavors complement the strong, salty, and spicy notes of Prästost. Alternatively, a robust white wine like a Chardonnay can also pair well, balancing the cheese's intensity with its buttery and oaky undertones.

In Swedish cuisine, Prästost is used in various traditional dishes. One popular recipe is "Prästost Soup," where the cheese is melted into a creamy soup, often served with crusty bread. Another famous dish is "Prästost Gratäng," a cheesy potato gratin that showcases the cheese's melting properties and enhances the dish's savory flavors.

99. Fontina

Italy | **Semi-Soft** | **Cow**

Fontina is a traditional Italian cheese produced in the Aosta Valley since the 1100s. This semi-cooked cheese is made from the raw milk of Valdostana Pezzata Rossa cattle. Depending on the length of maturation, Fontina's texture can vary from semi-soft to firm, while its flavor ranges from mild, sweet, and nutty to robust and quite tangy.

Fontina has a rich history, deeply embedded in the culture of the Aosta Valley. The cheese's production methods have been passed down through generations, maintaining its traditional characteristics. The Valdostana Pezzata Rossa cows graze on the rich alpine pastures, which imparts unique flavors to the milk and, consequently, the cheese.

One of the most famous uses of Fontina is in the traditional Valdostana style fondue, known as "Fonduta alla Valdostana." This creamy, rich dish showcases Fontina's excellent melting properties. Another classic dish is "Valpelline Soup," which combines Fontina with Lardo d'Arnad and hearty vegetables. "Costolette alla Valdostana" is yet another popular recipe, featuring breaded veal cutlets topped with melted Fontina.

For a delightful wine pairing, consider a Nebbiolo, particularly from the Barbaresco region. Nebbiolo's full-bodied structure, pronounced tannins, and complex notes of cherry, rose, and earthy truffle enhance Fontina's creamy texture and rich flavor. The wine's acidity cuts through the cheese's richness, creating a balanced and harmonious tasting experience that highlights the best qualities of both the wine and the cheese.

Fontina's versatility extends beyond traditional dishes. It can be melted over roasted vegetables, incorporated into creamy risottos, or used to elevate a simple sandwich. The cheese's ability to pair well with various ingredients makes it a staple in both everyday cooking and gourmet cuisine.

98. Dubliner

Ireland | **Hard** | **Cow**

Dubliner is a distinctive Irish cheese originating from County Cork, crafted from cow's milk. Renowned for its firm, smooth, and crystalline texture, Dubliner offers a unique flavor profile that combines nutty, sharp, and sweet notes, making it a favorite among cheese enthusiasts. The cheese is encased in a natural rind and is available today in a variety of flavors, catering to diverse palates.

John Lucey, the inventor of Dubliner, remains the guardian of its secret recipe, ensuring the cheese's unique qualities are preserved. His creation has gained widespread acclaim for its versatility and rich taste. Dubliner pairs exceptionally well with a glass of Cabernet Sauvignon or a pint of Guinness, enhancing its complex flavors. It also makes for a delightful addition to a simple yet satisfying meal when melted between slices of crusty brown bread.

Dubliner's popularity extends beyond its flavor, owing much to its versatile culinary applications. It is an excellent choice for cheese boards, where its distinct texture and taste can be fully appreciated. Additionally, it can be used in various recipes, adding depth and richness to dishes such as macaroni and cheese, quiches, and gourmet sandwiches.

An interesting fact about Dubliner is its creation in County Cork, a region celebrated for its rich agricultural heritage and high-quality dairy products. The cheese's natural rind and crystalline texture are a testament to the traditional cheesemaking techniques employed in its production.

Dubliner cheese embodies the best of Irish cheesemaking traditions, offering a taste that is both robust and refined. Its ability to complement both wine and beer makes it a versatile choice for various occasions, from casual gatherings to sophisticated tastings.

97. Sbrinz

Sbrinz is a Swiss extra-hard cheese made from raw cow's milk, known for its dense and flaky texture. It has a natural rind and offers slightly spicy aromas, while its flavors are full, intense, tangy, spicy, and nutty, with delightful notes of butterscotch.

Traditionally aged for at least 18 months, Sbrinz becomes more aromatic with age. It can be enjoyed in three distinct ways: when aged for 18 months, it is sliced or shaved into thin rolls; from 24 months and beyond, it is broken into smaller pieces called "möckli"; and when fully matured, it can be grated to enhance various dishes.

The history of Sbrinz dates back over 500 years to the central region of Switzerland. It is one of the oldest European cheeses, with references to its production appearing as early as the 16th century. The cheesemakers of Sbrinz have long adhered to traditional methods, ensuring the cheese's quality and distinctive flavor profile are maintained across generations.

For a perfect wine pairing, consider a Swiss white wine like a Fendant from the Valais region. Its crisp acidity and light fruitiness complement the nutty and tangy flavors of Sbrinz beautifully. Alternatively, a full-bodied red wine such as a Barolo or Amarone can also pair excellently, standing up to the cheese's intense and spicy notes.

In Swiss cuisine, Sbrinz is incredibly versatile. It can be shaved over salads or carpaccio, adding a flavorful punch to these dishes. One famous dish featuring Sbrinz is "Älplermagronen," a hearty Alpine macaroni and cheese where the cheese provides a rich, savory layer. Another popular recipe is "Zürcher Eintopf," a traditional stew where the cheese adds depth and complexity.

96. Caña de Cabra

Spain | **Semi-Soft** | **Goat**

Caña de Cabra is a renowned Spanish cheese from the mountainous region of Murcia, celebrated for its high-quality goat milk products. This soft-ripened goat milk cheese comes in a log shape and is a staple in Spanish cuisine. Young Caña de Cabra boasts a mild and creamy texture with refreshing lemony notes, while aged Caña de Cabra develops a sharp, intense flavor with a hint of earthiness.

The cheese has a rich history, rooted in the traditional cheesemaking practices of Murcia. The region's unique climate and terrain contribute to the distinct flavors of Caña de Cabra, making it a cherished product among cheese enthusiasts.

Caña de Cabra is typically enjoyed with local honey, figs, and almonds or pine nuts, creating a delightful balance of flavors and textures. Its creamy consistency and evolving flavor profile make it a versatile cheese for various culinary uses.

For a well-suited wine pairing, crisp white wines are recommended. A Spanish Albariño, with its bright acidity and citrus notes, complements the lemony undertones of young Caña de Cabra. Alternatively, a Sauvignon Blanc, known for its herbaceous and zesty profile, pairs beautifully with the sharper, aged version of the cheese.

In Spanish cuisine, Caña de Cabra is often featured in both simple and sophisticated dishes. One popular recipe is "Caña de Cabra Salad," where the cheese is paired with mixed greens, fresh figs, toasted almonds, and a drizzle of honey for a refreshing and flavorful dish. Another renowned dish is "Caña de Cabra Crostini," where slices of the cheese are melted over toasted baguette slices and topped with a touch of local honey or a sprinkle of fresh herbs.

95. Oscypek

Poland | **Semi-Hard** | **Sheep**

Oscypek is a distinctive spindle-shaped smoked cheese originating from the Tatra highlands in Poland. Crafted exclusively from salted and unpasteurized milk of the Polish mountain sheep, it sometimes includes a small addition of milk from the Polish Podgórska red cow breed. This traditional cheese is produced between May and September in Podhale, the southernmost region of Poland.

Renowned for its pronounced smokiness, Oscypek offers a unique salty and slightly sour flavor profile with subtle hints of chestnuts. The cheese is mildly piquant and best savored grilled, often accompanied by a dollop of cranberry marmalade. Its firm, rubbery texture and rich taste make it a versatile ingredient in various culinary delights.

Oscypek is commonly used in traditional Polish dishes, such as "Oscypek z żurawiną" – grilled Oscypek served with cranberry sauce. Another popular dish is "Oscypek w cieście" – Oscypek cheese wrapped in dough and baked until golden and crispy. The cheese also pairs wonderfully with hearty bread, sausages, and pickles, creating a harmonious blend of flavors.

For an authentic regional wine pairing, try serving Oscypek with a glass of Polish dry white wine, such as "Jutrzenka" from the Malopolskie region. This wine's crisp acidity and subtle fruit notes complement the cheese's smokiness and saltiness, enhancing the overall tasting experience.

Moreover, Oscypek holds a special place in Polish culture and traditions. It is often associated with highland shepherds and their age-old cheesemaking techniques passed down through generations. Recognized as a protected product by the European Union, Oscypek's unique qualities and regional significance continue to be celebrated by locals and visitors alike, making it a quintessential symbol of Poland's culinary heritage.

94. Tomme Des Pyrenees

France | **Semi-Hard** | **Cow**

Tomme des Pyrénées is a semi-hard, cow's milk cheese hailing from the Pyrénées region in France. This cheese must mature for at least 21 days before consumption, during which time it develops its distinctive character. Tomme des Pyrénées is wrapped in a distinguishable black wax coating, which acts as a seal to prevent air from entering, thereby halting the maturation process and preserving its unique flavors.

Renowned for its bold flavors, Tomme des Pyrénées has a rubbery texture and a buttery, salty, earthy taste. Slight hints of sourness and undertones of mushrooms, garlic, onions, peanuts, and beef bouillon emerge as the cheese melts in the mouth, creating a complex and satisfying flavor profile.

The history of Tomme des Pyrénées dates back centuries, with cheese production in the Pyrénées region being a long-standing tradition. This cheese has been crafted by local cheesemakers who have passed down their techniques through generations, ensuring that each wheel of Tomme des Pyrénées reflects the rich heritage and terroir of the region.

For a delightful wine pairing, consider wines from the Pyrénées region, such as a robust Madiran. The wine's tannic structure and dark fruit notes complement the big, bold flavors of the cheese. Alternatively, a strong ale, like a Belgian Dubbel, pairs wonderfully with Tomme des Pyrénées, balancing its earthy and savory notes with malty sweetness.

Tomme des Pyrénées is not only enjoyed on its own but also featured in various French dishes. One popular recipe is "Tartiflette Pyrénéenne," a gratin made with potatoes, bacon, onions, and melted Tomme des Pyrénées, creating a rich and hearty dish. Another famous use is in "Croustade," a savory pie filled with cheese, ham, and vegetables, showcasing the cheese's versatility and depth of flavor.

93. Saint Agur

France | **Soft** | **Cow**

Saint Agur is a distinguished French cheese originating from Auvergne, specifically the village of Beauzac. This rindless blue cheese is crafted from cow's milk and typically left to ripen in cellars for 60 days. The result is a cheese with sharp, spicy, and fruity flavors, accompanied by an intense, milky aroma.

The texture of Saint Agur is very creamy and smooth, which allows it to melt and spread exceptionally well. Its unique octagonal shape is reminiscent of the basalt stones found in Auvergne, paying tribute to its regional origins. Saint Agur is best served with figs, pears, and walnuts, or used in dips and sauces to enhance their flavors.

Saint Agur was first created in 1988 by the French dairy cooperative Bongrain. Despite its relatively recent creation compared to other traditional French cheeses, it quickly gained popularity due to its rich flavor and versatile uses in cooking.

For a delightful wine pairing, consider a Sauternes. This sweet white wine's honeyed notes and balanced acidity complement the sharp and spicy flavors of Saint Agur. Alternatively, a bold red wine like a Malbec can stand up to the cheese's intense profile, creating a harmonious balance of flavors.

Saint Agur is used in various famous dishes. One such dish is "Tarte au Saint Agur," a savory tart combining the cheese with caramelized onions and herbs. Another popular recipe is "Saint Agur Sauce," a rich and creamy sauce perfect for drizzling over steaks or pasta. Additionally, Saint Agur makes a luxurious addition to cheese boards, paired with fresh fruits, nuts, and crusty bread.

92. Queijo Minas

Brazil | **Semi-Soft** | **Cow**

Queijo Minas is a traditional Brazilian cheese renowned for its handmade craftsmanship and distinctive characteristics. Originating from the state of Minas Gerais, this cheese is made from raw cow's milk and is celebrated for its tender, spongy texture and moistness. The flavor profile of Queijo Minas is generally mild and slightly salty, though it can vary depending on the ripeness and specific region of production.

One of the cheese's most notable qualities is its versatility. Queijo Minas is commonly used in Brazilian cuisine, particularly in the preparation of sandwiches, pancakes, and pastries. Its mild flavor allows it to complement a wide range of ingredients, making it a favorite choice for both savory and sweet dishes.

In addition to its culinary uses, Queijo Minas pairs well with cold cuts, salads, and various vegetables, which develop intense flavors when cooked. The cheese's moist texture helps it blend seamlessly into recipes, enhancing dishes with its subtle taste and creamy consistency.

For wine pairing a crisp and refreshing Brazilian white wine like Chardonnay from the Serra Gaúcha region. The wine's acidity and fruity notes of green apple and citrus complement the mild tanginess and creamy texture of Queijo Minas, creating a balanced and refreshing tasting experience.

An interesting fact about Queijo Minas is its role in Brazilian food culture, where it is often enjoyed as a staple in daily meals and festive occasions. The cheese is produced in several varieties, including fresh and aged versions, each offering unique characteristics. The fresh version is soft and has a milder flavor, while the aged variety becomes firmer and develops a more pronounced taste.

91. **Kraftkar**

Norway | **Semi-Soft** | **Cow**

Kraftkar is a standout blue cheese from Norway that has captured global attention and acclaim. Produced by the small family-run dairy, Tingvollost, located in the village of Torjulvågen, Kraftkar achieved remarkable recognition when it was awarded the title of the world's best cheese at the 2016 World Cheese Awards in San Sebastián, Spain. This prestigious accolade was given after more than a hundred judges evaluated over 3,000 cheeses based on their color, texture, and flavor.

Kraftkar is made from cow's milk and is renowned for its exceptional texture and flavor profile. The cheese presents an initial crumbly texture that transitions to a soft, creamy consistency as it melts in the mouth. The blue mold is evenly distributed throughout, creating a visually striking appearance and a balanced, complex flavor. Its taste is robust, with rich, tangy notes characteristic of high-quality blue cheeses.

The name "Kraftkar," meaning "strongman," pays homage to the legendary farmhand Tore Nordbø, known for his impressive strength. This nod to local folklore adds a unique cultural dimension to the cheese's identity.

One exceptional pairing is with a dessert wine like Norwegian Eiswein (ice wine). The intense sweetness and concentrated fruit flavors of the Eiswein balance the strong, pungent notes of the Kraftkar, creating a harmonious and indulgent tasting experience. Additionally, an aquavit with its caraway and herbal notes can complement the cheese's complexity, providing a traditional and flavorful Norwegian pairing.

To fully appreciate Kraftkar, it is best enjoyed with crackers, walnuts, figs, and fruit jams, or even on its own. Its distinctive flavors and creamy texture make it a versatile cheese that stands out in any culinary setting, reinforcing its status as the world's best cheese. For cheese lovers, a taste of Kraftkar offers a remarkable journey into the rich cheesemaking traditions of Norway.

90. Tomme de Savoie

France | **Semi-Soft** | **Cow**

Tomme de Savoie is a traditional French cheese hailing from the regions of Savoie and Haute-Savoie. This uncooked, semi-soft cheese is easily recognizable by its distinctive gray rind, which is dotted with yellow and red spots. Made from cow's milk, Tomme de Savoie is the oldest cheese from the Savoie region, with its unique qualities reflecting the influence of the mountain climate.

The origins of Tomme de Savoie trace back to local peasants who ingeniously transformed their summer milk supplies into cheese to sustain them through the winter months. The cheese is produced from skimmed milk left over after the cream is drained to make butter, resulting in a relatively low fat content of around 40%. This practical approach to cheesemaking not only ensured food security but also created a cheese with a unique flavor profile and nutritional profile.

After maturing for 2 to 4 months, Tomme de Savoie develops a pliable yet firm texture. Its flavor is a delightful blend of nutty, grassy, and rustic notes, with subtle hints of mushroom and citrus, making each bite a nuanced experience. The aging process in the cool, humid conditions of the Savoie region's cellars contributes to its complex taste and characteristic rind.

Tomme de Savoie, pairs wonderfully with French wines. A classic pairing is with a white wine from the Savoie region, such as Apremont. This wine, made from the Jacquère grape, offers light, crisp acidity and notes of green apple, pear, and alpine flowers, which complement the cheese's nutty and earthy characteristics.

Historically, it was a staple in the diet of local farmers, and today it continues to be celebrated as a symbol of the region's rich culinary heritage. The cheese's name "Tomme" refers to a type of cheese made in the French Alps, highlighting its deep roots in the local cheesemaking traditions.

89. Boerenkaas

Netherlands | **Semi-Hard** | Cow, Goat, Sheep, Buffalo

Boerenkaas, Dutch for farmer's cheese, is a unique handmade cheese produced using unpasteurized, raw milk from the farm's own animals. This artisanal process means only a small percentage of Dutch cheeses can carry the Boerenkaas name. Unlike its factory-made counterparts, Boerenkaas is considered more a product of art than of science, reflecting the individuality of each farm.

There are four main variations of Boerenkaas, depending on the type of milk used: Goudse, Leidse, and Edammer Boerenkaas made from cow's milk, and Boerenkaas from goat's, sheep's, or buffalo's milk. Additionally, seeds, herbs, and spices can be added to enhance the flavor. The cheese is semi-hard with an intense flavor reminiscent of caramel, butterscotch, and cashews, making it suitable for pairing with beer and full-bodied red wines. The flavor is not consistent across all Boerenkaas cheeses, as they are made on different farms with varying soil types, adding an element of excitement in discovering the differences and uniqueness of each wheel.

The history of Boerenkaas dates back to the 1600s, when Dutch farmers began making cheese to preserve surplus milk. This practice evolved over centuries, with each farm developing its own techniques and recipes, leading to the rich diversity of flavors found in Boerenkaas today.

For a delightful wine pairing, Boerenkaas goes well with a full-bodied red wine such as Cabernet Sauvignon. The wine's tannins and dark fruit notes complement the cheese's rich, nutty flavors. Alternatively, a robust beer like a Belgian Dubbel pairs wonderfully, balancing the cheese's intensity with malty sweetness. In Dutch cuisine, Boerenkaas is featured in various dishes. One popular recipe is "Boerenkaas Fondue," where the cheese is melted with white wine and garlic, creating a rich and flavorful dip for bread and vegetables. Another favorite is "Boerenkaas and Apple Salad," combining the cheese's savory notes with the sweetness of fresh apples and a tangy vinaigrette.

88. Feta

Greece | **Soft** | **Cow, Goat**

Feta is the most famous Greek cheese, affectionately called "the princess of cheeses." It is made from sheep's milk or a mixture of sheep's and goat's milk, with the latter not exceeding 30%. Feta is produced in regions such as Macedonia, Thessaly, Thrace, Epirus, the Peloponnese, and Central Greece.

Traditionally, Feta is produced with non-pasteurized milk, although the use of pasteurized milk is now also permitted. The cheese is made in large square or triangle-shaped molds and preserved in wooden barrels or tin containers filled with brine to keep it fresh and maintain its acidity. The word "feta" means slice in Greek, a name derived from the shape the curd takes when cut. This white, rindless cheese contains about 7% salt, making it one of the saltiest cheeses. Feta's flavor is very intense and fresh, with a tangy and slightly creamy texture that makes it stand out among other cheeses.

The history of Feta dates back to ancient times. It is believed to have been made in Greece for over 6,000 years, with references to its production found in Homer's "Odyssey." The cheese has always been an essential part of Greek culinary culture, often featured in religious and festive occasions.

For a delightful wine pairing, Feta goes well with a crisp, acidic white wine like Assyrtiko. The wine's citrus notes and acidity complement the salty and tangy flavors of the cheese. Alternatively, Feta pairs wonderfully with ouzo, a traditional Greek anise-flavored spirit. Feta is most commonly consumed as it is, but it also features prominently in a variety of dishes. The famous Greek salad, "Horiatiki," combines Feta with tomatoes, cucumbers, olives, and red onions, creating a refreshing and flavorful dish. Another popular dish is "Spanakopita," a savory pastry filled with spinach and Feta, showcasing the cheese's versatility and rich flavor.

87. **Scamorza**

Italy | **Semi-Soft** | **Cow**

Scamorza is an Italian pasta filata cheese made from cow's milk. The cheese is distinctively shaped into two connected balls, one smaller than the other. Its texture is semi-soft, firm, and chewy, with flavors that are milky and smoky. These two balls of cheese are strung together to ripen for two weeks, a process that gives the cheese its name, meaning "beheaded" in Italian.

Scamorza can also be smoked, known as scamorza affumicata, which adds an extra layer of smoky flavor to the cheese. Often compared to mozzarella, Scamorza boasts a more creamy and sweet flavor profile and is significantly drier. Its texture and flavor make it a versatile cheese in cooking.

The history of Scamorza dates back to Southern Italy, particularly in regions like Campania and Apulia. The cheese has been produced for centuries using traditional methods, which have been passed down through generations. The name "scamorza" is thought to derive from the Italian word "scamozzare," meaning to remove a part, referring to the cheese's distinctive shape.

For a delightful wine pairing, Scamorza pairs well with a crisp white wine such as Pinot Grigio. The wine's acidity and lightness complement the cheese's creamy and smoky flavors. For a more robust pairing, try a Chianti; its bold flavors and tannins balance the cheese's richness.

In Italian cuisine, Scamorza is highly valued for its melting properties. It is often used in dishes such as "Scamorza al Forno," where the cheese is baked until golden and bubbly. Another famous recipe is "Pizza Scamorza," where the cheese is used as a topping, providing a deliciously smoky and creamy element. Scamorza is also popular in lasagne, adding depth and richness to the layers of pasta, sauce, and meat.

86. Bagoss

Italy | **Hard** | **Cow**

Bagoss is a unique Italian cheese produced in the small village of Bagolino, located in the Lombardy region. This cheese is crafted from the milk of Bruna Alpina cows. During the curd breaking process, saffron is added to the cheese, which gives it its distinctive straw-yellow color.

The cheese is aged for at least 12 months, but it can mature for up to 3 years, developing a smooth rind over time. The aromas of Bagoss are reminiscent of freshly cut grass, and its flavor is savory, slightly spicy, and piquant. To fully appreciate the subtle hints of chestnuts and walnuts, Bagoss should always be consumed at room temperature.

Bagoss has a rich history, with production dating back to the 15th century. The addition of saffron, a precious and rare spice, underscores the cheese's special status and deep connection to local traditions. This artisanal cheese has been passed down through generations, maintaining its unique characteristics and quality.

For a delightful wine pairing, Bagoss pairs beautifully with full-bodied aged red wines such as Barolo or Amarone. The robust flavors of these wines complement the cheese's savory and spicy profile. Additionally, young sparkling wines like Prosecco create a pleasing contrast with their fresh and effervescent qualities.

In Italian cuisine, Bagoss is highly versatile. It is often used as a filling for savory dishes such as stuffed pasta or vegetable gratins. One famous recipe featuring Bagoss is "Casoncelli alla Bagossa," a type of stuffed pasta from Lombardy. The cheese is also commonly grated over pasta, soups, or risottos, adding depth and complexity to these dishes. For a truly indulgent experience, let Bagoss slowly melt over a slice of piping hot polenta, allowing its rich flavors to meld with the creamy texture of the polenta.

85. Queijo de Coalho

Brazil | **Semi-Soft** | **Cow**

Queijo de coalho is a traditional cow's milk cheese from the northeastern regions of Brazil. This cheese is known for its firm, yet elastic texture and slightly yellow color. Queijo de coalho is often sold on sticks for roasting because it can withstand high temperatures without melting, making it a popular snack.

With a salty and acidic flavor, Queijo de coalho is an ideal treat on numerous Brazilian beaches, where it is usually grilled and sprinkled with oregano. Its ability to hold up well to grilling has made it a staple in Brazilian barbecue culture.

The history of Queijo de coalho dates back to the colonization period when Portuguese settlers brought cheesemaking techniques to Brazil. Over time, the recipe evolved to suit the local climate and available ingredients, resulting in the distinctive cheese enjoyed today.

For a delightful wine pairing, consider a Portuguese Vinho Verde. Its light, slightly effervescent nature and crisp acidity complement the salty and acidic flavors of Queijo de coalho. Alternatively, a New Zealand Sauvignon Blanc, with its bright citrus notes and refreshing acidity, pairs wonderfully with the cheese's grilled and savory profile.

In Brazilian cuisine, Queijo de coalho is featured in various traditional dishes. One famous recipe is "Espetinho de Queijo," where the cheese is skewered and grilled to perfection, often served with a sprinkle of herbs or a squeeze of lime. Another popular dish is "Queijo de Coalho com Mel," where the cheese is grilled and drizzled with honey, offering a delicious contrast of salty and sweet flavors.

Whether enjoyed on a beach or at a barbecue, Queijo de coalho provides a unique and delightful taste experience.

84. **Slovenska Parenica**

Slovakia | **Soft** | **Sheep**

Slovenská parenica is a traditional Slovakian cheese made from unpasteurized sheep's milk, specifically from the Wallachian, Cigaya, East Friesian, and improved Wallachian breeds. It can also be made using a mixture of raw sheep's and cow's milk, with at least 50% being sheep's milk.

This soft, steamed cheese is unique in its presentation, wound into two rolls connected in an S-shape or spiral, then steamed and lightly smoked. The rolls are bound with cheese strings or chains. Slovenská parenica has a smoky aroma with the characteristic smell of sheep's milk, and its taste is delicate, mild, and slightly salty.

The cheese's texture is elastic and supple, with fibers and threads on the interior, and its exterior is yellow to brown due to smoking and steaming. Originally produced around Zvolen and Brezno in the early 19th century, Slovenská parenica has now become popular throughout Slovakia.

For a wine pairing, consider a Riesling. The wine's crisp acidity and fruity notes complement the mild and slightly salty taste of Slovenská parenica. Alternatively, a Sauvignon Blanc with its herbaceous and zesty profile pairs beautifully with the cheese's smoky and delicate flavors.

In Slovak cuisine, Slovenská parenica is often used in various traditional dishes. One famous dish is "Parenica Salad," where the cheese is combined with fresh vegetables, herbs, and a light vinaigrette, creating a refreshing and flavorful appetizer. Another popular recipe is "Parenica Stuffed Peppers," where the cheese is melted inside sweet peppers, offering a delightful blend of smoky and sweet flavors.

83. Cabra Transmontano

Portugal | **Hard** | **Goat**

Queijo de Cabra Transmontano is a hard cheese made from the raw milk of Serrana breed goats. Goat cheese has long played an important role in the economy of the Bragança region, with many local families raising goats and producing cheese as their main source of livelihood.

The cheesemaking process begins with milking the goats and filtering the milk, which is then heated. The curd is salted and cured at a low temperature and high humidity. The resulting cheese is round with a semi-hard crust, and its texture is uniform, smooth, and white. It is a firm cheese with an intense, pleasant aroma and a slight spicy note. Transmontano cheese has a moisture content between 25% and 35%. It is typically enjoyed as is, popular either as an appetizer or after a meal with sliced bread. It pairs wonderfully with local red wine.

For a well-researched wine pairing, consider a Portuguese Douro red wine. The bold flavors and rich tannins of the Douro wine complement the intense and slightly spicy notes of the cheese. Alternatively, a Spanish Rioja, with its deep fruit flavors and balanced acidity, pairs excellently with Queijo de Cabra Transmontano, enhancing the cheese's complex taste.

In Portuguese cuisine, Queijo de Cabra Transmontano is often used in traditional dishes like "Queijo de Cabra Assado," where the cheese is baked with herbs and olive oil, creating a deliciously melted and flavorful appetizer. Another popular dish is "Salada de Queijo de Cabra," a fresh salad featuring the cheese, walnuts, and honey. Queijo de Cabra Transmontano not only reflects the rich culinary traditions of the Bragança region but also serves as a testament to the craftsmanship of local cheese producers. Its unique flavor and texture make it a cherished addition to Portuguese gastronomy.

82. Saint-Marcellin

France | Soft | Cow

Saint-Marcellin is a cheese made from full-fat cow's milk in the French regions of Drôme, Isère, and Savoie. Named after the town of Saint-Marcellin in the Isère region, this cheese has a rich history and is beloved for its distinctive flavors. Saint-Marcellin comes in two varieties: dry and soft. The dry variety, made according to local tradition, has a firm texture, while the soft variety is matured longer to develop more intense aromas and a creamier texture. When left at room temperature, the rind of the soft variety almost disappears.

Originally, Saint-Marcellin was made with goat's milk, but by the 13th century, cow's milk became more common due to the abundance of cattle in the region. This shift helped in creating the creamy texture and unique flavor profile that is now characteristic of Saint-Marcellin.

For a wine pairing, perfect match is with a light, fruity red wine such as Beaujolais, made from the Gamay grape. Beaujolais offers bright acidity, low tannins, and notes of red berries and subtle earthiness, which complement the delicate, creamy characteristics of Saint-Marcellin.

In the local cuisine, Saint-Marcellin is often featured in a variety of dishes. One popular dish is "Gratin Dauphinois with Saint-Marcellin," where the cheese is melted over sliced potatoes, creating a rich and flavorful gratin. Another local favorite is "Salad with Warm Saint-Marcellin," where the cheese is lightly warmed and placed on top of mixed greens, walnuts, and a light vinaigrette. It can also be enjoyed simply with a fresh baguette, crackers, or sliced fruit like apples and persimmons.

Saint-Marcellin, with its flavors, continues to be a cherished cheese in French cuisine. Whether enjoyed on its own, paired with a fine wine, or incorporated into traditional dishes, it offers a taste of the rich culinary of the regions of Drôme, Isère, and Savoie.

81. Selles-sur-Cher

France | **Soft** | **Goat**

Selles-sur-Cher is a soft cheese made from full-fat goat's milk, originating from the Western Sologne region, including the Cher area in France. This cheese is easily recognized by its distinctive rind, which is dusted with wood ash to develop unique mineral notes. The name 'Selles' refers to its disk shape.

The texture of Selles-sur-Cher is reminiscent of moist clay, and its flavor profile includes salty, goaty, nutty, and grass-like notes. As the cheese matures, the nutty flavor becomes more pronounced. When eaten with the rind, the cheese offers a more intense, sharper taste due to the ash and mold.

Historically, Selles-sur-Cher has been produced since the 19th century. It was originally made by farmers in the Sologne region who used the milk from their goats to create this cheese. The traditional method of coating the cheese with ash was used to protect it during the aging process, which also added to its distinctive flavor.

For wine pairings, Selles-sur-Cher goes well with white wines. A light Sancerre complements the cheese's earthy flavors. The acidity of this wine balances the richness of the cheese, creating a harmonious pairing. Additionally, pairing it with a crisp Chardonnay can also be a good match, highlighting the cheese's unique characteristics. Serving the cheese with fresh fruits like pears or apples can further elevate the tasting experience.

In local cuisine, Selles-sur-Cher is often featured in various dishes. Tarte aux Chèvres et Tomates: A savory tart made with Selles-sur-Cher cheese, tomatoes, and herbs, baked to perfection with a flaky crust. Crostini au Chèvre et Miel: Toasted baguette slices topped with Selles-sur-Cher cheese and a drizzle of honey, often served as an appetizer. Quiche aux Chèvres et Épinards: A quiche made with Selles-sur-Cher, spinach, and eggs, baked until golden brown.

80. Caciocavallo Silano

Italy | **Semi-Hard** | **Cow**

Caciocavallo Silano is one of the oldest and most typical spun curd cheeses of Southern Italy. It originated from the Sila Plateau, with the tradition of cheesemaking gradually expanding along the Apennine mountain range. This cheese is produced in the regions of Basilicata, Calabria, Campania, Molise, and Apulia. Made from cow's milk, Caciocavallo Silano boasts a mild, salty flavor and a smooth, firm texture.

As Caciocavallo Silano ripens, its flavors become more pungent and its texture more granular, making it ideal for grating. The cheese's name is derived from "cacio," meaning cheese, and "cavallo," referring to the method of maturing: cheeses are hanged in pairs over a cavallo, a type of wooden saddle rack.

The history of Caciocavallo Silano dates back to ancient times, with references to its production found in texts from as early as the 5th century BC. The unique aging process, where the cheeses are hung in pairs, has been passed down through generations, ensuring the preservation of its traditional qualities.

For a well-matched wine pairing, consider a robust red wine like a Primitivo from Puglia. The wine's bold flavors and rich tannins complement the pungent and salty notes of aged Caciocavallo Silano. Alternatively, a dry white wine like a Vermentino can also pair well, balancing the cheese's saltiness with its crisp acidity and fruity undertones.

In Italian cuisine, Caciocavallo Silano is used in a variety of dishes. One famous recipe is "Parmigiana di Melanzane," where slices of eggplant are layered with tomato sauce, basil, and grated Caciocavallo, then baked until bubbly and golden. Another popular dish is "Caciocavallo alla Brace," where thick slices of the cheese are grilled until slightly melted and served with fresh bread and vegetables.

79. Liliputas

Lithuania | **Semi-Hard** | **Cow**

Liliputas is a handmade, semi-hard, naturally ripened cheese from the village of Belvederis in Lithuania. Made from pasteurized cow's milk, this cheese boasts a very high fat content of 50% and must mature for at least one month in cheese cellars. The cheese is wrapped in cotton cloths and pressed into cylindrical molds, giving it its distinctive shape and texture. The name Liliputas is derived from its small size and weight, typically ranging between 0.4 to 0.7 kilograms. The exterior of the cheese is smooth and thin, with a waxy rind. It has a firm yet elastic texture and an acidic, fresh, slightly sharp, and salty flavor, typical for a fermented cheese. The interior is creamy to pale yellow in color, and its unique production process makes it twice the price of mechanically produced cheeses. However, for consumers who appreciate the labor-intensive craftsmanship, Liliputas is a true delicacy.

Liliputas has a rich history rooted in Lithuanian cheesemaking traditions. The village of Belvederis has been known for its high-quality dairy products, and the meticulous process of creating Liliputas has been passed down through generations. This cheese is a testament to the dedication and skill of Lithuanian cheesemakers.

For an ideal pairing, Liliputas, gose well with a traditional Lithuanian beer, such as Švyturys Ekstra, a pale lager. The beer's crisp, clean taste and light malt sweetness complement the mild and smooth texture of Liliputas. Additionally, pairing Liliputas with Midus, a traditional Lithuanian mead, provides a delightful contrast as the honeyed sweetness and floral notes of the mead enhance the cheese's subtle flavors.

In Lithuanian cuisine, Liliputas is often enjoyed on its own or as part of a cheese platter. It is also used in various dishes to enhance their flavors. One popular recipe is "Liliputas Stuffed Mushrooms," where the cheese is melted inside mushroom caps, creating a deliciously creamy and savory appetizer. Another famous dish is "Liliputas Cheese Tart," where the cheese is incorporated into a rich and flavorful tart.

78. Formaella Arachovas

Greece | **Semi-Hard** | **Goat, Sheep**

Formaella Arachovas Parnassou is a semi-hard cheese made from goat's or sheep's milk, or sometimes a mix of the two. This cheese has been produced in the town of Arachova, below Mount Parnassus in central Greece, for over a century. The milk comes from animals that live in the mountains and eat local herbs and plants, giving the cheese its unique flavor.

The cheese-making process involves curdling the milk and then dividing the curd into special molds or baskets. These are then salted and dried on reed mats, which give the cheese its striped appearance. Formaella Arachovas Parnassou is known for its compact structure, cylindrical shape, and pale yellow color. It has a pleasant taste and aroma and is usually enjoyed plain or cooked, often fried or grilled, in various regional dishes.

Historically, Formaella has been a staple in Greek cuisine, cherished for its flavor and versatility. It is commonly used in dishes like "saganaki," a popular Greek appetizer where the cheese is fried until golden, and "tiropita," a savory cheese pie. Another well-known dish featuring Formaella is "boureki," a Cretan specialty consisting of layers of cheese, zucchini, and potatoes, baked until tender and flavorful.

For wine pairing, Formaella pairs excellently with Moschofilero, a white wine from the Peloponnese region. Moschofilero is known for its aromatic profile, featuring notes of citrus, white flowers, and a hint of spice, with a crisp acidity that complements the cheese's rich texture and tangy flavor. The wine's floral and citrus elements provide a refreshing contrast to the savory characteristics of Formaella Arachovas.

Formaella Arachovas Parnassou also has cultural significance. It is often featured in local festivals and celebrations, showcasing the region's rich agricultural traditions. The cheese is a source of pride for the people of Arachova.

11. Raclette de Savoie

France		Semi-Soft		Cow

Raclette de Savoie is an ancient mountain cheese hailing from the Savoie region in France and the canton of Valais in Switzerland. Its name comes from the French word "racler," meaning to scrape, which reflects the traditional method of serving this cheese.

This semi-soft cow's milk cheese is unpasteurized, featuring a dark-beige, slightly sticky rind, and a light yellow interior. Raclette de Savoie has a mild, pleasant flavor that becomes exceptionally delicious when heated. Traditionally, people would cut a large wheel of Raclette in half, place it near an open fire, and wait for the cheese's surface to melt and become golden brown. They would then scrape the melted cheese onto baked potatoes, creating a rich and nutty dish.

Raclette de Savoie pairs perfectly with baked potatoes, but it also complements cooked and cured meats. Today, you can recreate this traditional dish by heating slices of Raclette under a grill. In the canton of Valais, it's common to enjoy Raclette with tea, while in Savoie, people often pair it with white wine, such as Vin de Savoie. For an international twist, Raclette also pairs beautifully with a crisp Sauvignon Blanc or a Riesling, which enhances the cheese's nutty aroma.

Historically, Raclette de Savoie has been enjoyed for centuries by shepherds and farmers in the Alps, who would melt the cheese over an open fire during cold mountain evenings. Over time, it has become a beloved dish across Europe.

Famous dishes made with Raclette de Savoie include the traditional Raclette, where the cheese is melted and scraped over potatoes, and Croque-Monsieur Raclette, a twist on the classic French sandwich using Raclette cheese. Another popular dish is Raclette Fondue, combining melted Raclette with various dipping options like bread, vegetables, and meats.

76. Gorgonzola Dolce

Italy | **Soft** | **Cow**

Gorgonzola Dolce DOP is a soft, high-moisture blue cheese originating from the Piedmont and Lombardy regions of Italy. Crafted from pasteurized cow's milk, this cheese undergoes a 45-day aging process in warm rooms. It is characterized by its delicate blue and green veining and is known for being milder than its counterpart, Gorgonzola Piccante DOP.

The texture of Gorgonzola Dolce is luxurious, creamy, and spreadable, making it perfect for a variety of culinary uses. Its flavor profile is milky and mildly piquant, with sweet, nutty undertones that come from its oozing paste and blooming blue veins. The aromas are mild and milky, contributing to its overall creamy, sweet, and buttery taste.

Historically, Gorgonzola cheese has been produced for over a thousand years, with its origins tracing back to the town of Gorgonzola in the Lombardy region. It is one of the oldest blue cheeses in the world, and over the centuries, the method of production has been refined to create the delicious Gorgonzola Dolce we know today.

For a delightful pairing, enjoy Gorgonzola Dolce with fresh fruits, honey, and slightly sweet sparkling wines. A glass of Vin Santo or Champagne complements the cheese perfectly, enhancing its creamy and sweet characteristics. Alternatively, you can pair it with a light Moscato d'Asti or a fruity Riesling for an equally delightful experience.

Gorgonzola Dolce is versatile in the kitchen and is featured in many famous dishes. It can be spread on crusty bread, stirred into risottos for a rich, creamy texture, or used as a topping for pizzas and flatbreads. One popular dish is Gorgonzola Dolce and Pear Crostini, where the cheese is paired with ripe pear slices on toasted bread, drizzled with honey for a perfect balance of flavors. Another favorite is Gorgonzola Dolce Pasta, where the cheese is melted into a sauce with cream and tossed with pasta for a luxurious meal.

75. Morbier

France | Semi-Soft | Cow

Morbier cheese, a semi-soft cow's milk cheese, originates from the Franche-Comté region in eastern France. Traditionally, this cheese featured a layer of ash in the middle, used to separate the morning and evening milk curds during its making. Today, Morbier is crafted from a single milking, and the ash line is often replaced with vegetable dye to maintain its visual tradition. The cheese is typically aged for 45 days, during which it develops a creamy texture with flavors that range from fruity and grassy to slightly citrusy. Some producers also extend the aging period to 100 or even 150 days, intensifying its flavor profile.

The history of Morbier dates back to the 19th century, when cheesemakers in Franche-Comté used leftover curds to make a smaller cheese. They would sprinkle ash over the morning curds to protect them until the evening curds were added, creating the characteristic line. This practical solution has evolved into a unique visual and flavor element of Morbier.

Morbier is a cheese that works well in many different dishes. It's delicious on sandwiches, pairs nicely with crackers, nuts, and grapes, and melts smoothly into hot dishes. For a truly satisfying pairing, enjoy Morbier with a light red wine like Beaujolais or a white wine such as a crisp, unoaked Chardonnay from Burgundy. These wines complement the cheese's creamy texture and slightly tangy flavor, creating a delightful balance.

Famous dishes featuring Morbier include the classic French raclette, where the cheese is melted and scraped over boiled potatoes, pickles, and cured meats. Morbier also shines in a cheese fondue, mixed with other Alpine cheeses, providing a rich and flavorful dip for bread and vegetables.

74. Époisses

France | **Soft** | **Cow**

Époisses de Bourgogne, commonly known as Époisses, is a soft cheese made from raw cow's milk in the village of Époisses in Burgundy, France. This cheese matures for at least six weeks, during which it develops a complex texture and taste that cheese enthusiasts find delightful. With a creamy and firm consistency, Époisses is easily recognized by its distinctive red-orange color, a result of its unique ripening process.

One of the most intriguing aspects of Époisses is its strong aroma, which has led to its ban on public transport in France. This smear-ripened cheese is washed in Marc de Bourgogne, a potent brandy from the Burgundy region, which imparts a pungent, spicy flavor. The natural, brick-red glossy rind forms as it matures, contributing to its unmistakable character. To maintain its shape and contain its gooey texture, Époisses is traditionally sold in a wooden box.

Époisses has a rich history dating back to the 16th century when Cistercian monks in Burgundy first began its production. The recipe was passed down through generations, with local farmers continuing the tradition. In the 1950s, the Berthaut family revived the cheese, preserving its heritage and ensuring its place in French culinary culture.

In terms of culinary use, Époisses is best enjoyed with a slice of crusty bread, allowing its creamy texture and bold flavor to shine. It pairs exceptionally well with a glass of white wine, such as Chablis, which complements the cheese's richness with its crisp acidity. Alternatively, a Belgian Dubbel can balance the strong flavors of Époisses, creating a harmonious taste experience.

Famous dishes featuring Époisses include the classic French tartiflette, where the cheese is melted over potatoes, bacon, and onions. Its creamy consistency also makes it a luxurious addition to sauces and gratins, enriching the overall flavor profile.

73. Paški sir

Croatia | **Hard** | **Sheep**

Paški sir is a hard cheese from Croatia, originating from the island of Pag. This cheese is made from the milk of the Pag sheep, which graze on the island's herbs such as immortelle, sage, and sea fennel, all flavored by the salty bura wind. This unique environment imparts a distinct flavor to the milk, and consequently to the cheese.

This award-winning cheese is characterized by its dry, flaky, grainy, and crumbly texture, coupled with a tangy, salty flavor. During its production, Paški sir is typically rubbed with ash and olive oil before being left to mature for at least four months. As it ages, its tangy and savory flavors intensify, making it a favorite among cheese enthusiasts. When young, Paški sir has a herby and salty taste, reminiscent of Manchego in both texture and flavor. As it matures, it develops a more robust profile similar to Pecorino Romano.

Paški sir is best served at room temperature, sliced into triangles. The aged version pairs excellently with fruit jams, olive oil, wildflower honey, anchovies, prosciutto slices, grapes, or local bread rolls known as paške bubice. However, locals advise against using it in sandwiches. The younger version of the cheese is versatile for culinary use; it can be shaved on top of risottos and pasta dishes or melted to create a rich pasta sauce. To store Paški sir, it is recommended to place it on a wooden board, turning it occasionally while rubbing it with olive oil to prevent drying out and mold development.

During the Homeland War in Croatia from 1991 to 1995, cheese production continued despite the lack of electricity for 26 months, with refrigeration relying on natural outdoor conditions.

For wine pairings, Paški sir goes wonderfully with a red wine like Zinfandel, which complements the cheese's intense flavors. Famous dishes featuring Paški sir include "Paški Sir Risotto," where the cheese is shaved over creamy risotto.

12. Y Fenni

Wales | **Semi-Hard** | **Cow**

Y Fenni is a distinctive Welsh cheese crafted from a blend of mature Cheddar, wholegrain mustard, and Welsh ale. Known for its easy melting properties, Y Fenni is often placed on steaks for the final grilling, adding a flavorful, spicy touch without being overbearing. The cheese is typically coated in either red or yellow wax, which helps preserve its rich flavor and smooth texture.

The name Y Fenni comes from the Welsh name for Abergavenny, a market town renowned for its production. This unique cheese has its roots in the tradition of combining local ingredients to create a product that reflects the culinary heritage of the region. The inclusion of wholegrain mustard and Welsh ale gives Y Fenni its characteristic spicy flavor, making it a standout addition to any cheese board.

For a delightful wine pairing, consider a full-bodied red wine like a Shiraz. The bold flavors and spicy notes of the Shiraz complement the mustard and ale-infused Y Fenni, creating a harmonious balance. Alternatively, a crisp, refreshing white wine like a Sauvignon Blanc can also pair well, cutting through the richness of the cheese.

In addition to being a popular component of the traditional ploughman's lunch, Y Fenni is used in various dishes. One famous recipe is "Y Fenni Cheese Sauce," where the cheese is melted into a creamy sauce perfect for drizzling over vegetables or pasta. Another popular dish is "Y Fenni Grilled Cheese Sandwich," where the cheese's melting qualities shine, creating a deliciously gooey and flavorful treat.

Y Fenni's unique flavor and versatility make it a cherished cheese in Welsh cuisine. Its spicy yet balanced taste profile, combined with its local heritage, offers a delightful experience for cheese enthusiasts. Whether enjoyed as part of a hearty ploughman's lunch, melted over a steak, or incorporated into a comforting grilled cheese sandwich, Y Fenni brings a taste of Wales to any table.

11. Slovenský Oštiepok

Slovakia | **Semi-Hard** | **Sheep, Cow**

Slovenský oštiepok is a traditional semi-hard cheese made from half-fat sheep's milk, cow's milk, or a mixture of both. It can be steamed or unsteamed, smoked or unsmoked, and produced either industrially in dairies or traditionally on sheep farms (salaš) in Slovakia's mountainous regions. Its striking appearance, resembling a large egg or pine cone, features a golden brown exterior from the smoking process and a creamy yellow interior.

The texture of Slovenský oštiepok is firm and homogeneous, with small cracks appearing when sliced. Its taste is delicate and savory, with hints of saltiness, sourness, and a distinctive smoky flavor.

Historical records and family archives of early cheese makers confirm that Slovenský Oštiepok PGI has been produced since the early 18th century. While industrial production began around 1921, it wasn't until the 1960s and 1970s that cheese making became standardized and included the use of cow's milk.

When it comes to wine pairings, Slovenský oštiepok goes well with a crisp dry white wine such as a Sauvignon Blanc. The wine's acidity complements the cheese's smoky and slightly piquant flavors. Alternatively, a light Pilsner beer can also be a good match, balancing the cheese's savory notes.

Famous dishes featuring Slovenský oštiepok include "Grilled Oštiepok," where the cheese is grilled until slightly melted and served with bread or vegetables. Another popular dish is "Oštiepok Salad," combining the cheese with fresh greens, tomatoes, and a light vinaigrette, offering a delightful mix of textures and flavors. "Baked Oštiepok with Potatoes" is another traditional favorite, where the cheese is baked with sliced potatoes and herbs, creating a comforting and flavorful meal.

70. Pecorino Siciliano

Italy | **Hard** | **Sheep**

Pecorino Siciliano is one of the oldest cheeses in Europe, with a rich history dating back thousands of years. This semi-cooked, hard cheese is made from raw, whole milk from various sheep breeds across Sicily. It's easily recognizable by the unique reed-woven basket pattern on its rind.

The cheese is known for its herbal aroma and well-balanced, piquant flavor, which becomes stronger as it ages. There are several varieties of Pecorino Siciliano, including Tuma, Primo Sale, Secondo Sale, and Stagionato. Fresh and semi-matured versions are typically enjoyed with bread and olives, while the aged types are perfect for grating over pasta.

Pecorino cheese boasts a deep-rooted history in Italy, tracing its origins back to ancient Rome. It served as a fundamental sustenance for shepherds and farmers in rural regions. The name "Pecorino" is derived from the Italian word for sheep, "pecora," highlighting that this cheese is crafted from sheep's milk. Over the centuries, Pecorino cheese has become a beloved food in Italy and around the world.

For wine lovers, Pecorino Siciliano pairs wonderfully with red wines like Nero d'Avola and light white wines such as Grillo. These wines complement the cheese's flavors, making for a delightful tasting experience.

In the kitchen, Pecorino Siciliano is a versatile ingredient. One famous dish that features this cheese is Pasta alla Norma, a classic Sicilian pasta dish with eggplant, tomatoes, and basil. The grated Pecorino adds a savory kick that brings the dish together. Another popular use is in Caciocavallo Ragusano, a Sicilian cheese-filled pastry, where Pecorino Siciliano's flavor shines through.

69. Stracciatella

Italy | **Soft** | **Buffalo**

Stracciatella is a delightful Italian cheese originating from the Puglia region. This unique cheese is the creamy filling of burrata, made from shredded threads of mozzarella di bufala, or sfilacci, mixed with fresh cream. The result is a silky, buttery, and almost runny texture, with flavors that are fresh, milky, and slightly acidic.

Stracciatella has a fascinating history. It evolved as a way to use leftover mozzarella curds, blending them with cream to create a rich, creamy delicacy. This cheese has been a staple in Italian cuisine for many years, gaining popularity for its versatility and delectable taste. The word means "little rag" in Italian, describing the torn look of the cheese. It was created in the 1920s in Andria, a town in Puglia, southern Italy.

For wine enthusiasts, Stracciatella pairs wonderfully with light and crisp white wines such as Vermentino. This wine complement the cheese's fresh and slightly tangy flavors, creating a harmonious pairing.

In the kitchen, Stracciatella is incredibly versatile. It can be used in a variety of dishes, from appetizers to main courses. Pizza Burrata: A gourmet pizza topped with Stracciatella and fresh basil. Pasta alla Stracciatella: A pasta dish featuring Stracciatella cheese, cherry tomatoes, and fresh basil. Insalata di Pomodori e Stracciatella: A tomato salad with Stracciatella, olive oil, and balsamic vinegar. Stracciatella can be enjoyed simply spread on a piece of crusty bread or as a topping for bruschetta. Its mild flavors make it a perfect companion to both savory and sweet dishes, allowing for endless culinary creativity.

Store freshly made stracciatella in a sealed, airtight plastic or glass container in the coldest part of your refrigerator for up to four days. In Italy, it is best enjoyed within 48 hours of production. If you have access to freshly made stracciatella, try to consume it as soon as possible for the best flavor.

68. Cabécou

France | Soft | Goat

Cabécou is a delightful soft goat milk cheese hailing from the Midi-Pyrenees region of southern France. This cheese has a unique preparation process that makes it stand out. First, it is dipped in plum brandy, which gives it a distinct flavor. Then, it is sprinkled with coarse black pepper and wrapped in two chestnut leaves for maturation. This method of maturation adds to its rich taste and creamy texture.

Historically, Cabécou has been produced in this region for centuries. The traditional methods of its production have been passed down through generations, maintaining the authentic taste that cheese lovers adore. The name "Cabécou" actually comes from the old Occitan language, meaning "little goat," reflecting its origin and main ingredient.

Cabécou has a thin striped rind that develops a blue mold after two weeks of aging. Its smooth, creamy texture and calm cream color make it visually appealing. The flavor is slightly tangy, with a subtle hint of brandy, offering a unique tasting experience.

When it comes to wine pairing, Cabécou pairs exceptionally well with Chardonnay from Burgundy. The wine's crispness and slight acidity balance the creamy and buttery notes of the cheese perfectly. This combination highlights the unique flavors of both the cheese and the wine, making for a delightful culinary experience.

This cheese is versatile in the kitchen and can be used in various recipes, such as: Cabécou Tart: Spread caramelized onions over the puff pastry, top with slices of Cabécou, sprinkle with thyme, drizzle with honey, and season with salt and pepper. Bake until the pastry is golden and the cheese is melted. Grilled Cabécou with Honey and Herbs: Brush the Cabécou with olive oil and sprinkle with fresh herbs, salt, and pepper. Grill until the cheese is warm and slightly melted. Drizzle with honey before serving.

67. Manchego curado

Spain | **Semi-Hard** | **Sheep**

Manchego curado is a well-known Spanish cheese made from sheep's milk. This variety of Manchego cheese is aged from 3 to 6 months, placing it in the third stage of aging. The texture of Manchego curado is semi-firm, smooth, and creamy, making it a favorite among cheese enthusiasts. Its flavors are mild and pleasant, with sweet, nutty, caramel-like notes and a slight piquant finish.

Manchego cheese has a long history in Spain, originating from the La Mancha region. This area has a rich tradition of sheep farming, and the cheese is made exclusively from the milk of Manchega sheep. The distinct flavor and quality of Manchego curado are a result of both the specific breed of sheep and the unique aging process.

One of the key features of Manchego curado is its excellent melting properties, which make it a popular choice in various dishes. It is often used in quesadillas, where its creamy texture and nutty flavor shine. Manchego curado can also be grated over salads, melted into sauces, or served as part of a cheese platter.

For wine pairings, Manchego curado goes well with both red and white wines. A good match is a Spanish red wine like Tempranillo, which complements the cheese's sweet and nutty flavors. A dry white wine such as Albariño also pairs nicely, balancing the slight piquancy of the cheese.

Manchego curado is used in many traditional Spanish dishes. One famous dish is "Manchego and quince paste," where the cheese is paired with sweet quince jelly, creating a delightful contrast of flavors. Another popular dish is "Croquetas de Manchego," crispy croquettes filled with creamy Manchego cheese. The cheese is also enjoyed simply sliced with olives and cured meats, a common way to start a Spanish meal.

66. Picón Bejes-Tresviso

Spain | **Semi-Hard** | **Cow, Sheep, Goat**

Picón Bejes-Tresviso is a traditional blue cheese from Cantabria, in the north of Spain. Made from a blend of cow's, sheep's, and goat's milk, this cheese is renowned for its distinctive flavor and unique production process. The curds, roughly the size of hazelnuts, are loosely placed in molds, which allows air to circulate and encourages the growth of Penicillium mold, essential for developing the cheese's blue veins.

After molding, the cheese is salted and dried for 12 to 18 days at a temperature between 15 and 18 °C (59 and 64 °F). This process results in a thin rind that ranges in color from grey to yellow-green. Inside, the cheese is white, smooth, and compact, with striking teal-colored veins running throughout. The flavor of Picón Bejes-Tresviso is powerful, with a slightly spicy and tart taste.

The history of Picón Bejes-Tresviso is deeply rooted in the small villages of Bejes and Tresviso. The cheese was traditionally made in mountain caves, where the cool and humid conditions were ideal for aging blue cheese. These natural caves provided the perfect environment for the development of the Penicillium mold, which is essential for creating the cheese's unique flavor and texture.

For wine pairings, Picón Bejes-Tresviso pairs exceptionally well with red wines like Rioja or Ribera del Duero, which complement the cheese's strong flavors. Sweet wines such as Pedro Ximénez can also be a great match, as their sweetness balances the cheese's tartness and spice.

In Spanish cuisine, Picón Bejes-Tresviso is often enjoyed as a table cheese, served with bread and fresh fruit. It is also used in various dishes, such as salads and sauces, where its intense flavor adds depth and complexity.

65. Kasseri

Greece | **Semi-Hard** | **Sheep, Goat**

Kasseri is a renowned semi-hard Greek cheese with a rich heritage, traditionally crafted from sheep's milk, with the occasional addition of up to 20% goat milk. Originating from the regions of Macedonia, Thessaly, and the Xanthi and Lesvos prefectures, Kasseri has been a staple in Greek cheese-making since the 19th century, embodying the essence of traditional dairy practices.

To meet regulations, Kasseri must ripen for at least three months, but it is typically left to mature for six to twelve months. Younger Kasseri has a delicate, sweet, and tangy flavor, while aged versions develop a salty and piquant taste, somewhat resembling Parmesan cheese.

Kasseri belongs to the pasta filata family, known for cheeses with a stretchy texture like mozzarella. Its pale yellow color and slightly sweet aftertaste come from the sheep milk used in its production. Kasseri has a mild, milky taste and a buttery texture, making it an excellent table cheese.

In Greek cuisine, Kasseri is enjoyed in various ways. It is commonly sliced for sandwiches or used as a topping on pizzas. Traditional Greek dishes featuring Kasseri include "Pita Kaisarias," a savory pie filled with kasseri and pastrami; "Kasseri Tiganismeno," where the cheese is pan-fried; and "Saganaki," a popular appetizer where the cheese is fried until golden and crispy.

For a delightful wine pairing, consider a Greek Assyrtiko. This white wine's crisp acidity and citrus notes complement the sweet and tangy flavors of younger Kasseri. For aged Kasseri, a full-bodied red wine like a Spanish Tempranillo, with its rich fruit flavors and balanced tannins, pairs excellently.

64. Melichloro

Greece | **Hard** | **Goat, Sheep**

Melichloro is a traditional Greek cheese produced on the island of Lemnos. Made from a blend of fresh sheep's and goat's milk, this cheese boasts a hard texture and rich, complex flavors that capture the essence of the island's herbs and wildflowers.

Melichloro cheese matures in dark, dry rooms, particularly during late spring when humidity is at its lowest, ensuring optimal drainage and flavor development. This careful process results in a hard cheese ideal for grating over various dishes. The tradition of cheese-making on Lemnos dates back to ancient times, with Melichloro being a staple in the local diet due to its long shelf life and nutritional value.

Melichloro pairs well with both ouzo and tsipouro, traditional Greek grape distillates. The herbal and aniseed notes of ouzo complement the cheese's sharpness, providing a balanced taste experience. Similarly, tsipouro offers a strong, rich character that works well with Melichloro's intensity, with its complex, slightly fruity notes blending harmoniously with the cheese. Both distillates, with their distinct profiles, elevate the taste of Melichloro, creating a satisfying and authentic Greek pairing.

Two popular Greek dishes made with Melichloro cheese are Melichloro Saganaki and Melichloro Stuffed Peppers. Melichloro Saganaki features slices of the cheese, lightly coated in flour and pan-fried until golden and crispy on the outside, while remaining soft and melty on the inside, often served with a squeeze of lemon juice. Melichloro Stuffed Peppers consist of bell peppers filled with a mixture of grated Melichloro cheese, rice, herbs like dill and parsley, and sometimes ground meat, then baked until tender. These dishes highlight Melichloro's sharp and savory flavors, showcasing its versatility in both appetizers and main courses.

63. Myzithra

Greece | **Soft** | **Goat, Sheep**

Myzithra is a traditional Greek cheese made from the whey of goat's or sheep's milk cheeses. This versatile cheese comes in three main varieties: fresh, sour, and aged. The fresh variety is soft in texture, unsalted, and typically shaped into eggs or balls. Its aroma is pungent, while the flavor is quite mild, making it ideal for various culinary uses.

Sour Myzithra is prepared with sheep's or goat's milk, yeast, and salt, resulting in a slightly tangy flavor and a firmer texture compared to the fresh variety. The aged variety of Myzithra is hard in texture and very salty, known for its crumbly consistency and robust flavor.

The history of Myzithra dates back to ancient Greece, where it was mentioned in classical texts and enjoyed by the likes of Aristotle and Homer. Traditionally, Myzithra was a way to utilize the leftover whey from the production of other cheeses, ensuring no part of the milk was wasted.

Fresh and sour Myzithra are often used in baked pastries and desserts, adding a delicate flavor and creamy texture. A famous dish featuring these varieties is "Kalitsounia," sweet Cretan pastries filled with Myzithra and flavored with honey and cinnamon. Another popular dish is "Bougatsa," a filo pastry filled with Myzithra, semolina, and sugar. The aged Myzithra, with its intense saltiness, is best when grated over pasta, soups, and casseroles. It is often used in traditional Greek dishes such as "Pasta with Aged Myzithra," where the cheese is sprinkled generously over freshly cooked pasta, or "Moussaka," where it is used to top the baked layers of eggplant, meat, and béchamel sauce.

For a wine pairing, consider a dry Italian Pinot Grigio pairs well with the fresh and sour varieties, enhancing their delicate flavors without overpowering them.

62. Provola

Italy | **Soft** | **Cow**

Provola is an Italian cheese that can be considered a smaller version of Provolone. Made from cow's milk, this cheese originates from the Campania region. Provola is a pasta filata cheese, which means it undergoes a process where the curds are stretched and kneaded. Typically, the cheese is immersed in brine, and some varieties are smoked (known as Provola affumicata) before being hung to dry for at least four months.

The flavors of Provola can range from mild and sweet to very sharp, depending on the aging period and the specific region of production. Apart from the plain and smoked varieties, Provola can also be found in various elongated shapes. The name "Provola" is derived from "pruvula" or "pruvatura," referring to an ancient tradition where priests at the convent of San Lorenzo in Capua were offered cheese on a piece of bread as proof of its quality.

Provola pairs well with wines that complement its range of flavors. For a mild Provola, a light and crisp white wine such as Pinot Grigio works well, highlighting the cheese's subtle sweetness. For the sharper, aged varieties, a bold red wine like Chianti provides a good balance, bringing out the cheese's complex flavors.

In Italian cuisine, Provola is a key ingredient in various dishes. It is often enjoyed as a table cheese but also shines in cooked recipes. On pizza, Provola often replaces mozzarella, providing a unique flavor and texture. In lasagna, it adds depth and richness, melting beautifully between layers of pasta and sauce. Risottos with Provola are creamy and flavorful, with the cheese melting into the rice to create a luscious dish. Additionally, Provola is a great choice to bruschettas, where its flavor complements the fresh toppings.

61. Ladotyri Mytilinis

Greece | **Hard** | **Goat, Sheep**

Ladotyri Mytilinis is a hard table cheese traditionally crafted on the island of Lesbos, located in the Northern Aegean Islands of Greece. This cheese is made from sheep's milk or a combination of sheep's and goat's milk, with the latter never exceeding 30%. Its production in special cylindrical molds gives Ladotyri Mytilinis its distinctive shape and pale yellow color.

The cheese is known for its salty and slightly spicy flavor, accompanied by a fragrant aroma characteristic of sheep's milk. After maturing, Ladotyri Mytilinis is commonly preserved in olive oil or covered with paraffin wax, a method reflected in its name, which translates to "the cheese preserved in oil."

Ladotyri Mytilinis has a rich history rooted in the island of Lesbos, where it has been made for centuries. It is highly esteemed both locally and across Greece, despite being one of the rarer cheeses available on the market.

For an optimal tasting experience pair Ladotyri Mytilinis with Assyrtiko for its citrusy acidity, Xinomavro for its spicy, smokey notes, Barbera for its high acidity and cherry flavors, or Furmint for its spicy aromatics and orchard fruit. These wines enhance the cheese's rich, tangy profile perfectly

In Greek cuisine, Ladotyri Mytilinis is versatile and enjoyed in various dishes and salads. One popular dish is Ladotyri Saganaki, where the cheese is pan-fried until golden and served with lemon wedges. Another favorite is the Ladotyri Mytilinis and Tomato Salad, combining fresh tomatoes, herbs, and olive oil with chunks of this flavorful cheese. The cheese also shines when grated over pasta or baked into savory pies, adding a distinctive taste and aroma.

60. Brie de Melun

France | Semi-Soft | Cow

Brie de Melun is a historic French cheese, often regarded as the ancestor of all Brie varieties. Originating in the Seine-et-Marne region of northern France, this cheese has been cherished for centuries and holds a special place in French culinary heritage. It received AOC (Appellation d'Origine Contrôlée) protection in 1980, ensuring its production follows strict guidelines to maintain its supreme quality.

Made from unpasteurized cow's milk, Brie de Melun is produced in the areas of Aube and Yonne and the Brie region of Île-de-France. Compared to its more famous cousin Brie de Meaux, Brie de Melun is smaller, yet it boasts a stronger and saltier taste. The cheese has a golden yellow body encased in a white, moldy rind with reddish streaks, making it visually distinct. It requires a longer production and maturation period of 4-8 weeks, allowing its unique flavors to develop fully.

The flavor profile of Brie de Melun is rich and complex. It has a fruity and musty taste, with hints of straw that add to its depth. Its aroma is aromatic, with slightly musty and straw-like scents that float in the air, enhancing the tasting experience. As the cheese ages, the rind becomes darker and crumbly, transforming into a Brie Noir, which has an even stronger taste and a drier, darker interior. The cheese's texture is semi-soft, and the rind is slightly dry. The flavors are strongly lactic and slightly salty, finished by soft, barnyard, and sour notes.

Brie de Melun is a versatile cheese and is often used in regional dishes like croûte au brie. It pairs wonderfully with bread and pears, providing a delightful balance of flavors. When it comes to wine pairings, Brie de Melun shines with lighter red wines that won't overpower its delicate flavors. Excellent choices include Gaillac and wines from Burgundy or the Rhone Valley. For an international touch, consider pairing it with a Beaujolais from France or a Pinot Noir from California, both of which complement the cheese beautifully.

59. Manchego fresco

Spain | **Semi-Hard** | **Sheep**

Manchego fresco a beloved Spanish cheese, hails from the La Mancha region, renowned for its rich dairy tradition. Made exclusively from the milk of Manchega sheep, this cheese is celebrated for its unique flavor and texture, which varies with age. Available in several varieties, Manchego includes Fresco (fresh and mild, aged for just two weeks), Semi Curado (aged three weeks to three months, semi-firm with a fruity, tangy flavor), Curado (aged three to six months, offering subtle caramel and nutty notes), and Viejo (aged one to two years, firm, crumbly, and intensely flavorful with peppery undertones). The cheese is easily recognizable by its distinctive basket-weave rind pattern, a nod to its traditional production methods.

The taste and texture of Manchego fresco cheese evolve as it ages. Younger Manchego is creamy and mild, with hints of fresh grass and herbs, while aged Manchego develops richer, nuttier, and more complex flavors. Its texture transitions from semi-soft and slightly crumbly to firm and compact, enhancing its versatility in culinary applications. This cheese is a staple in many dishes, whether enjoyed on cheese platters paired with cured meats, olives, and fruits, or melted in grilled sandwiches, quesadillas, and baked dishes. It also adds depth and creaminess to salads and sandwiches when shaved or grated and complements sweet fruits and honey in desserts.

For an excellent pairing, Manchego fresco cheese pairs beautifully with a glass of Tempranillo or a bold Cabernet Sauvignon. These wines enhance the cheese's nutty and caramel flavors, creating a delightful combination for cheese lovers. Historically, Manchego's origins trace back to Roman times, making it a cheese with a storied past. Its production has remained largely unchanged, preserving its traditional taste and cultural significance. Famous dishes featuring Manchego fresco include traditional Spanish tapas, cheese-stuffed peppers, and even innovative desserts that showcase its unique flavor profile.

58. Sfela

Greece | **Semi-Hard** | **Goat, Sheep**

Sfela is a cherished semi-hard cheese traditionally produced from sheep or goat milk, or a mixture of the two. The milk used to make this cheese comes from breeds reared in the Messinia and Lakonia prefectures of Greece, where Sfela has been produced for over a century.

The cheesemaking process for Sfela involves dividing the curd into pieces and reheating them. These pieces are then drained using cheesecloth, lightly pressed, and cut into small strips known as 'sfelas.' These strips are salted and stored in tin cans full of brine for at least three months to mature. During this maturation period, Sfela develops its characteristic yellowish color and a body full of small holes created during fermentation.

Sfela has a robust, tangy flavor and a firm texture, making it a beloved ingredient in modern Greek cooking. It is usually served as an appetizer, often grilled to enhance its slightly salty and rich taste. Sfela is also popular in various Greek dishes, such as "Sfela Saganaki," where the cheese is pan-fried until golden and crispy, and "Sfela Pie," combining the cheese with meat and vegetables in a savory pastry.

The history of Sfela dates back to over a century ago, with local cheesemakers in Messinia and Lakonia perfecting their techniques to produce this distinctive cheese. The traditional methods and the unique environment of these regions contribute to Sfela's unique flavor and quality.

For a well-researched wine pairing, consider a Greek white wine like Assyrtiko. Its crisp acidity and citrus notes beautifully complement the tanginess and saltiness of Sfela, creating a harmonious balance of flavors. Alternatively, a French, Picpoul de Pinet known for its vibrant acidity and herbaceous notes, can also pair well with the cheese.

57. Mastelo

Greece | Semi-Soft | Cow, Goat

Mastelo is a trademarked Greek cheese produced exclusively on the island of Chios. It comes in two varieties: one made from Chian cow's milk and the other from goat's milk. The cow's milk version is characterized by its white color, milky aroma, and smooth texture. This cheese offers slightly salty and milky flavors, and its high melting point makes it excellent for grilling. It is particularly well-suited for saganaki, a popular Greek fried cheese meze.

The goat's milk variety of Mastelo also has a white color but features a soft and elastic texture with a distinctly salty flavor. This version is often used as a substitute for mozzarella in pizzas and pies. It can also enhance sandwiches or serve as a stuffing in a variety of meat and vegetable dishes. Mastelo is traditionally paired with Greek ouzo, which complements its salty and milky notes.

The history of Mastelo cheese is deeply rooted in the island of Chios. The name "mastelo" refers to a wooden bucket traditionally used for collecting milk, highlighting the cheese's connection to local dairy farming practices. Over time, the production of Mastelo has evolved, yet it remains a cherished product of the island, reflecting Chios's rich agricultural heritage.

Mastelo is great for many culinary uses. It shines when grilled due to its high melting point, making it ideal for Greek dishes like saganaki. It also adds a unique Greek twist to pizzas and works well in pies, where its creamy texture and mild flavor blend smoothly with different fillings.

For pairing Mastelo cheese, consider a crisp Sauvignon Blanc, a dry Rosé from Provence, or a light Pinot Noir. These wines' acidity and fruitiness complement the tangy, slightly crumbly texture of Mastelo, providing a delicate complement to the cheese's flavors.

56. Queijo Serpa

Portugal | **Semi-Soft** | **Sheep**

Queijo Serpa, a semi-soft sheep's milk cheese, is produced in the district of Beja in eastern Portugal. Similar to Pecorino, Serpa stands out due to its unique curdling process, which uses an extract made from a species of thistle that grows in the Alentejo countryside. The thistle leaves are dried and soaked in water, and this liquid is then added to heated milk to begin the curdling process. The resulting curd is placed into molds, wrapped gently in muslin cloth, and left to ripen. The cheese develops a thin, malleable rind, while its interior remains semi-soft and yellowish-white.

Serpa is the most famous traditional cheese of the Alentejo region and holds a special place in the cultural heritage of Portugal. Its strong, distinctive flavor is cherished, making it an excellent choice for various occasions. Serpa is perfect as an appetizer or snack when served with fresh bread and a glass of wine. Its robust taste also makes it a versatile ingredient in numerous local baked dishes, such as pork ribs with baked ham and Serpa cheese.

Cheese making in this region has deep historical roots. Although the techniques originated from the Serra de Estrela, they have evolved to fit the natural resources and climate of the Alentejo region. The earliest written mention of this cheese is from 1905, in a document by Joaquim Rasteiro for the Congresso de Leitaria.

When it comes to pairing, Queijo Serpa goes wonderfully with a full-bodied red wine like Alentejo's own Trincadeira, which complements the cheese's strong flavors. A crisp white wine such as a Portuguese Vinho Verde also provides a refreshing contrast to the richness of Serpa.

Famous dishes featuring Queijo Serpa highlight its versatility and depth of flavor. One popular recipe is "Entrecosto no forno com Queijo Serpa" (oven-baked pork ribs with Serpa cheese), where the cheese adds a creamy, tangy layer to the savory dish.

55. Sir iz Mijeha

Bosnia & Herzegovina | **Soft** | **Sheep, Cow**

Sir iz mijeha is a unique cheese from Herzegovina, traditionally encased in a large sheepskin sack. This cheese is made from raw sheep's milk, cow's milk, or a combination of both. The sheep's milk comes from the Pramenka breed, while the cow's milk is sourced from Busa and Gatacko breeds. The size of the sheepskin sack determines the cheese's size, which can weigh anywhere from 30 to 70 kilograms.

The cheese is aged for a period ranging from two months to a year, during which it develops a white or pale yellow color. Sir iz mijeha is known for its strong aroma of sheepskin, a testament to its traditional preparation methods. The flavor is robust and distinct, making it a cherished part of Bosnian cuisine. This cheese is typically served as an appetizer, often accompanied by boiled potatoes, ham, and uštipci (fried dough), which enhance its savory profile. To store Sir iz mijeha, it is recommended to keep it in a cool, dry place, preferably wrapped in a cloth or wax paper to maintain its moisture and prevent it from drying out.

The history of Sir iz mijeha is deeply rooted in Bosnian and Herzegovinian pastoral traditions. The use of sheepskin sacks for aging cheese dates back centuries, reflecting the resourcefulness and ingenuity of local shepherds. This method not only imparts a unique flavor but also preserves the cheese naturally, making it an integral part of the region's culinary heritage.

For an exquisite pairing, consider Žilavka, a white wine from Herzegovina known for its fresh acidity and citrus, apple, and stone fruit notes. The wine's acidity and freshness balance the cheese's richness, while its citrus elements provide a refreshing contrast to the tangy flavors, creating a harmonious and delightful tasting experience. In terms of culinary applications, Sir iz mijeha is often featured in traditional Bosnian dishes. One popular dish is "Sir iz Mijeha Pita," a savory pie filled with layers of cheese and phyllo dough, offering a delicious combination of textures and flavors.

54. Old Amsterdam

Netherlands | **Hard** | **Cow**

Old Amsterdam is a Dutch Gouda-style cheese made from pasteurized cow's milk. This cheese undergoes maturation in three stages, each bringing out specific characteristics in flavor and texture. Master cheesemakers carefully monitor the wheels, determining the optimal time for consumption based on these qualities. The result is a cheese with a hard, smooth texture dotted with occasional eyes and tiny granular crystalline pieces of amino acids. Its paste resembles the color of butterscotch, while the flavors are sweet, rich, toasty, nutty, robust, and caramel-like.

Old Amsterdam was officially launched in the Netherlands in 1985. It quickly gained popularity among cheese enthusiasts both at home and abroad. Today, the cheese continues to win numerous international awards. Gouda cheese has been crafted in this region for hundreds of years, with recipes and methods handed down through generations. Old Amsterdam was created to embody the rich character of aged Gouda while maintaining a consistent quality and taste. This has made it a beloved choice not only in the Netherlands but also around the world.

Old Amsterdam is great for many different uses. Its rich flavor works well with figs, pistachios, and salads. It can be shredded over soups, used in sandwiches, or enjoyed on its own. For a perfect pairing, try Old Amsterdam with a full-bodied red wine like Cabernet Sauvignon or a smooth, rich white wine such as Chardonnay. The cheese's sweet and nutty notes match well with the wine, creating a balanced taste experience.

Famous dishes featuring Old Amsterdam include "Old Amsterdam Cheese Fondue," where its melting qualities and rich flavor make a tasty dipping sauce for bread and vegetables. Another favorite is "Old Amsterdam and Fig Salad," which combines the cheese's nuttiness with the sweetness of figs. Additionally, the "Old Amsterdam Grilled Cheese Sandwich" upgrades the classic sandwich with its deep flavors and creamy texture.

53. Tête de Moine

Switzerland | **Semi-Hard** | **Cow**

Tête de Moine AOP, translating to "Monk's Head," is a distinctive Swiss cheese originating from the Jura region. This semi-hard, unpasteurized cow's milk cheese is celebrated for its unique presentation and rich flavor. Traditionally, it is served using a special tool called a "girolle" to shave thin rosette-like curls from the cheese wheel, which enhances its aroma and taste. The cheese boasts a dense, creamy texture and a nutty, slightly spicy flavor.

The name "Tête de Moine" has been known since 1790, but its origins trace back to the 12th century. The canons at Bellelay monastery were first recorded making Tête de Moine AOP as early as 1192, over 825 years ago, which was a century before the Swiss Confederation was established. Tête de Moine was used as a form of payment, highlighting its value and significance. This ritualistic preparation adds a sensory experience to its consumption, making it a centerpiece in both flavor and presentation.

Tête de Moine goes well with crisp white wines like Pinot Grigio and Chardonnay. These wines' light and refreshing qualities match the cheese's rich, nutty flavors and slightly spicy notes. Its creamy texture works nicely with these wines. Alternatively, a light red wine such as Pinot Noir or a dry sparkling wine like Champagne or Prosecco provides a pleasant contrast, making for a balanced taste experience.

Tête de Moine is great in many dishes. One popular option is "Tête de Moine Rosettes with Fresh Fruit," where the cheese curls are served with slices of apple, pear, and grapes, bringing out the cheese's nutty and spicy notes. Another favorite is "Tête de Moine Cheese Fondue," where the cheese is melted and used as a rich and creamy dip for bread and vegetables. Also, "Tête de Moine Salad" features the cheese rosettes on fresh greens with nuts and a light vinaigrette, creating a tasty mix of flavors and textures.

52. **Metsovone**

Greece | **Semi-Hard** | **Cow, Goat, Sheep**

Metsovone is a Greek cheese with a distinctive smoky flavor, produced in the mountainous region of Metsovo. This hard or semi-hard table cheese is traditionally made from cow's milk or a blend of cow's milk with up to 20% sheep's or goat's milk. The cheese has been a staple in the Metsovo area for over 50 years, made using milk from local animals.

The process of making Metsovone involves several steps. The milk is poured into cylindrical molds and placed in cold water to help the cheese become compact. After this, the cheese is brined, and then it undergoes a maturation period of at least three months. The final step is smoking the cheese for a couple of days, which gives Metsovone its unique flavor.

Metsovone has a textured paste and a slightly yellow rind. Its taste is rich, with a slightly salty and spicy note, and it finishes with a dried fruit aftertaste. This cheese is versatile, enjoyed both raw and cooked. It is a common ingredient in quiches and pizzas, and it is an excellent appetizer, often served with a glass of ouzo or wine.

For wine pairings a Syrah or a Cabernet Sauvignon works well due to their boldness, which matches the cheese's intense smokiness. For a white option, a Chardonnay with some oak aging complements the cheese's richness and smokiness without overwhelming it. These wines provide the right contrast and depth to make the most of Metsovone's unique taste, offering a harmonious balance between the cheese's flavors and the wine's characteristics.

In Greek cuisine, Metsovone is featured in various dishes. One popular dish is saganaki, where the cheese is pan-fried to create a golden crust. Metsovone also melts well, making it a great choice for grilled cheese sandwiches or as a topping for baked pasta dishes.

51. Gruyère

Switzerland | **Hard** | **Cow**

Gruyère is a well-known Swiss cheese made from raw cow's milk. This cooked and pressed cheese features a grainy rind that ranges from yellow to brown, while its interior boasts a creamy ivory to pale yellow color. The Swiss version, known as Gruyère AOP, is a hard cheese with a salty and nutty flavor, typically without holes. In contrast, the French version, Gruyère IGP, is characterized by holes that can be as small as a pea or as large as a cherry.

The cheese-making process for Gruyère is very precise, requiring at least 120 days of maturation in cellars. During this period, the cheese develops its signature aromas of caramelized apples, hazelnuts, and brown butter. This aging process is essential for achieving the complex flavors that Gruyère is famous for.

Gruyère has a rich history, originating from the town of Gruyères in the canton of Fribourg, Switzerland. Cheese production in this region dates back to at least the 12th century, with Gruyère being officially recognized and protected under Swiss law. The cheese has since become a staple in Swiss cuisine and is celebrated worldwide.

One of the most famous dishes made with Gruyère is the classic Swiss fondue. Gruyère's excellent melting properties make it ideal for this dish, where it is combined with other cheeses, white wine, and garlic to create a creamy and flavorful dip. Gruyère is also a key ingredient in French onion soup, adding depth and richness to the dish when melted on top of croutons.

For wine pairings, Pinot Noir or a Merlot is a great match, as their fruitiness and moderate tannins balance the cheese's flavors without overwhelming them. For white wine, a dry Riesling or a Sauvignon Blanc works well, providing a crisp contrast that cuts through the cheese's creaminess. These choices offer a good balance, allowing the distinct notes of Gruyère to shine while also creating a pleasant taste experience.

50. Sulguni

Georgia | **Semi-Hard** | **Cow, Goat, Buffalo**

Sulguni is a traditional Georgian cheese that originates from the Samegrelo (Mingrelia) region. This cylindrical cheese has a mild yet complex flavor profile and a semi-firm texture. Sulguni can be made from the milk of cows, buffalos, and occasionally goats, or a combination of these milks.

The flavor of Sulguni varies depending on its type. Fresh Sulguni has a tangy, acidic, and slightly sour taste, while the smoked and semi-hard varieties introduce salty and smoky notes. Its specific flavor makes it a popular choice in many dishes, and it melts easily, making it an excellent pizza topping. Sulguni is also commonly added to salads and pasta dishes, where it complements a variety of ingredients.

Sulguni has a rich history in Georgian cuisine. The cheese-making tradition in Samegrelo dates back centuries, with local methods passed down through generations. This cheese is an integral part of Georgian culture and is often made in family-run dairies that uphold traditional practices.

Pairing Sulguni with wine can bring out its flavors. A crisp white wine like Rkatsiteli pairs well with the tangy and acidic notes of fresh Sulguni. For smoked or semi-hard varieties, a medium-bodied red wine such as Saperavi is a good match, complementing the cheese's smoky and salty flavors.

In Georgian cuisine, Sulguni is featured in various famous dishes. One notable dish is Khachapuri, a popular cheese-filled bread where Sulguni's melting properties are showcased. Another traditional dish is Sulguni grilled on skewers, served hot with a crispy exterior and a gooey interior. Sulguni is also enjoyed simply sliced and served with fresh vegetables and herbs, making it a versatile ingredient in Georgian meals.

49. Arseniko Naxou

Greece | **Semi-Hard** | **Sheep, Goat**

Arseniko Naxou is a traditional Greek cheese from the island of Naxos, with its name "arseniko" meaning male or masculine. This cheese is crafted from raw sheep's and goat's milk, with whey added during the process.

The production of Arseniko Naxou involves several steps. Once the milk thickens, the cheese is drained in specially designed baskets known as tirovola. Initially, Arseniko Naxou has a sweet flavor, but as it matures over a few months, it develops a spicy and aromatic taste. The texture also changes, becoming firmer and more crumbly with time.

Arseniko Naxou has a tradition spanning a thousand years, with its history documented in the village of Koronos. The traditional methods of making this cheese have been passed down through generations, preserving its unique character and regional significance. The island's lush pastures and diverse flora contribute to the distinct flavors found in the cheese.

Arseniko Naxou, pairs wonderfully with Moschofilero, a white wine from the Peloponnese region. Moschofilero is known for its aromatic profile, featuring notes of rose petals, citrus, and a hint of spice, along with bright acidity. The wine's floral and citrus elements complement the tangy and slightly salty characteristics of Arseniko Naxou. This pairing creates a refreshing and harmonious tasting experience that showcases the distinctive flavors of Greek cuisine.

Arseniko Naxou is used in various Greek dishes. One famous dish is "Sfougato," a type of omelette made with eggs, zucchini, and Arseniko Naxou, highlighting the cheese's rich flavor. Another popular dish is "Pitarakia," small cheese pies made with Arseniko Naxou and herbs, perfect for a savory snack or appetizer. The cheese can also be grated over pasta or salads, adding a spicy kick and aromatic depth.

48. Taleggio

Italy | **Semi-Soft** | **Cow**

Taleggio is an Italian cheese made from cow's milk, known for its soft, creamy texture and strong aroma. It has a fruity flavor and a thin rind that ranges from rosy to orange, which may develop edible mold as it ages. Produced in square blocks, Taleggio becomes ready for consumption after 40 days of aging, during which its pungent aroma intensifies.

The origins of Taleggio trace back to the Alpine valley of Val Taleggio, where it has been produced since Roman times. Initially, it was made exclusively in Val Taleggio, but by the late 1800s, production expanded to other regions in northern Italy, including Lombardia, Piemonte, and the province of Treviso in Veneto. The cheese ages in cold and humid environments, with the rind regularly treated with water and salt to develop its distinctive appearance and flavor.

When pairing wine with Taleggio, both red and white wines can be great choices. A light red like Valpolicella pairs well, as its subtle fruitiness matches the cheese's strong and savory notes. On the other hand, a white wine such as Chardonnay complements the cheese's creamy texture and gentle flavor, offering a smooth contrast. These combinations bring out the best in Taleggio, making for a balanced and enjoyable pairing.

Taleggio can be enjoyed on its own but is also widely used in cooking due to its excellent melting properties. It adds a rich and creamy texture to various dishes. One popular dish is risotto with Taleggio, where the cheese is melted into the rice to create a smooth and flavorful consistency. Taleggio is also used in polenta, giving the dish a creamy melt and unique taste. It works well in grilled cheese sandwiches, offering a deliciously gooey filling.

47. Gorgonzola piccante

Italy | **Semi-Soft** | **Cow**

Gorgonzola piccante is a traditional Italian blue cheese made from pasteurized cow's milk. Known for its distinctive sharp, strong, and intense flavors, this cheese offers a creamy yet crumbly texture with blue veins running throughout its paste. The natural moldy rind encases its spicy and pungent aromas, setting it apart from the milder Gorgonzola dolce variety.

The history of Gorgonzola dates back to the Middle Ages, originating in the town of Gorgonzola near Milan. Over the centuries, this cheese has become a staple in Italian cuisine, renowned for its rich and bold taste. Gorgonzola piccante is aged for a minimum of 80 days, during which it develops its characteristic sharpness and complexity.

Gorgonzola piccante pairs exceptionally well with various beverages. Rum, port, and mead are particularly good choices, as their sweetness and strength complement the cheese's intense flavors. The contrast between the sharpness of the cheese and the sweetness of these drinks creates a balanced and enjoyable tasting experience.

In Italian cuisine, Gorgonzola piccante is used in a variety of dishes. One famous dish is Gorgonzola sauce, often served with pasta or gnocchi. The cheese melts smoothly, creating a rich and flavorful sauce. Another popular dish is Gorgonzola-stuffed figs or pears, where the intense flavor of the cheese contrasts beautifully with the sweetness of the fruit. Additionally, it can be crumbled over salads, adding a burst of flavor, or included in a cheese platter alongside nuts and honey.

Gorgonzola piccante is also enjoyed on its own, perhaps with a slice of crusty bread and a glass of one of the recommended beverages. Its bold flavors and creamy texture make it a standout cheese that captures the essence of Italian cheesemaking tradition.

46. Kefalotyri

Greece | **Hard** | **Goat, Sheep**

Kefalotyri is a traditional Greek-Cypriot cheese made from goat's or sheep's milk. This cheese has a firm and flaky texture with irregular holes and a strong, rich aroma. Its flavor profile is salty, strong, tangy, sharp, and spicy.

The origins of Kefalotyri trace back to the Byzantine era, making it one of the oldest hard cheeses in Greece. It is believed to be the predecessor of many other hard Greek cheeses. Kefalotyri comes in two main varieties: young Kefalotyri, which is aged for a minimum of 2-3 months, and aged Kefalotyri, which is aged for at least one year and has a much stronger flavor.

For wine pairings, Kefalotyri pairs excellently with Agiorgitiko, a red wine from the Nemea region. Agiorgitiko offers soft tannins, moderate acidity, and flavors of red fruits like cherry and raspberry, along with a hint of spice. The wine's fruitiness and balanced acidity complement the sharp and tangy characteristics of Kefalotyri, while its smooth tannins provide a nice counterpoint to the cheese's firmness. This pairing enhances the complexity of both the cheese and the wine, creating a harmonious and delightful tasting experience that showcases the richness of Greek gastronomy.

Kefalotyri is highly valued in Greek cuisine for its role in various dishes. It is commonly used in pasta and meat dishes, grated over stews, salads, and pizzas to add a rich, tangy flavor. One famous Greek dish featuring Kefalotyri is "Saganaki," where the cheese is fried until it forms a crispy crust on the outside while remaining soft inside. This dish showcases the cheese's ability to withstand high heat and bring out its natural flavors. Kefalotyri is also used in baked dishes such as "Moussaka" and "Pastitsio," where it is grated over the top to create a golden, flavorful crust. It is often served as an appetizer, drizzled with olive oil and sprinkled with oregano. The cheese's firm texture makes it easy to slice and grill, providing a delightful addition to any meal.

45. Livanjski sir

Bosnia & Herzegovina | **Hard** | **Cow, Sheep**

Livanjski sir is a traditional Bosnian cheese first produced in 1886, modeled after Swiss and French cheese-making techniques. Initially, it was made exclusively with sheep's milk, but over time, the production methods evolved. Today, many industrially produced varieties use only cow's milk, while some local, family-owned businesses still use a combination of sheep's and cow's milk.

This hard cheese typically ripens for sixty to eighty days, although it can age for longer to develop a deeper flavor. Depending on the aging process, Livanjski sir can range in color from pale to dark yellow. Its texture remains hard yet elastic, with evenly distributed, medium-sized holes. The cheese is known for its strong flavors and pleasant, nutty aromas.

In 1933, over 20 cheese productions were documented in Livno and its surroundings. The Banovina Cattle stations in Livno and on Cincar mountain, the pioneers in cheese production, were particularly notable. "Livanjski sir" production was estimated at 20 to 30 wagons per year. Most of the cheese was sold in Split, with exports also reaching Belgium, France, and South America.

For wine pairings, Livanjski sir is best enjoyed with Herzegovinian wines lsuch as Žilavka and Blatina. These full-bodied wines complement the strong and nutty flavors of the cheese, creating a balanced and satisfying tasting experience. Besides wine, the cheese pairs well with smoked meats, which highlight its rich and complex taste.

In Bosnian cuisine, Livanjski sir is often served as an appetizer. It is sliced and presented alongside smoked meats, olives, and fresh bread. The cheese is also used in various dishes, such as traditional pies and pastries, where its flavor adds depth and character.

44. Bryndza Podhalańska

Poland | **Soft** | **Sheep, Cow**

Bryndza Podhalańska is a unique soft cheese made from the milk of the Polska Owca Górska (Polish Mountain Sheep) breed, produced in the Nowotarski, Tatrzański, and some parts of the Żywiecki districts in Poland. This cheese can also be made with a mixture of sheep's and cow's milk, provided the cows are of the Polska Krowa Czerwona (Polish Red) breed, with the cow's milk comprising no more than 40% of the total mixture. Bryndza Podhalańska gets its name from the traditional region of Podhale, where many skilled cheesemakers produce this delicacy.

The cheese has a white, creamy-white, or greenish color and offers an intense, salty, and slightly sour flavor. It is a seasonal product made only from May until September. The unique flora of one of Europe's cleanest regions greatly influences the quality of this fresh and creamy cheese.

For wine pairings, Bryndza Podhalańska, a several Polish wines make excellent pairings. A Młode Wino (young wine) offers a light, fruity profile that contrasts nicely with the cheese's sharpness. A Chardonnay from the Łaskotki region brings bright acidity and subtle fruitiness that complements the cheese's creamy texture. A Riesling from the Ziemia Lubuska region provides a crisp and slightly sweet balance to the cheese's tangy notes. Additionally, a French Pinot Noir with its light and fruity characteristics, pairs well without overwhelming the cheese.

In Polish cuisine, Bryndza Podhalańska is used in various traditional dishes. One popular dish is "Oscypek with Bryndza," where slices of the semi-hard Oscypek cheese are paired with Bryndza for a delightful contrast in textures and flavors. Another local favorite is "Bryndza Pierogi," dumplings filled with a mixture of Bryndza and potatoes, creating a rich and savory filling. The cheese is also enjoyed simply spread on fresh bread with a sprinkling of chives or herbs, offering a simple yet flavorful snack.

43. San Michali

Greece | **Hard** | **Cow**

San Michali is a hard cheese made exclusively from the milk of cows bred on the island of Syros in the Cyclades archipelago. This famous cheese has been produced for over half a century using the same traditional methods. The local cows are fed a diet of aromatic local plants and herbs, which contribute to the buttery scent of this cheese. It is quite hard and compact with many irregular holes.

San Michali has a cylindrical shape and its color ranges from light to intense yellow. The cheese has a unique aroma and a pleasantly spicy taste with an aftertaste reminiscent of dried fruit. It can be eaten plain as a table cheese, and it is also often used as an ingredient in soufflés or omelettes.

San Michali's history dates back to the mid-20th century when dairy farmers on Syros sought to create a unique cheese that reflected the island's rich flora and traditional cheesemaking techniques. Over time, San Michali has become a beloved staple in Greek cuisine and a symbol of the island's culinary heritage.

For a delightful wine pairing, consider a Greek Assyrtiko from Santorini. The wine's crisp acidity and citrus notes complement the spicy and fruity flavors of San Michali. Alternatively, a Chardonnay with its buttery and slightly oaky profile can enhance the cheese's rich and aromatic qualities.

San Michali is often featured in various Greek dishes. One popular recipe is "San Michali Soufflé," where the cheese adds a rich and creamy texture to the dish. Another favorite is "San Michali Omelette," where the cheese is melted into fluffy eggs, creating a savory and satisfying meal.

San Michali is a testament to the rich cheesemaking tradition of Syros, offering a unique flavor profile that reflects the island's natural beauty and culinary heritage.

42. Queso Payoyo

Spain | **Semi-Hard** | **Sheep, Goat**

Queso Payoyo is a distinctive Spanish cheese made from a blend of milk from Payoyo goats and Grazalema sheep, both native to the region of Andalusia. Known for its rich and tangy flavor, Queso Payoyo has a creamy, softer texture compared to Manchego, with a recognizable cross-hatched rind. The cheese carries subtle aromas of butter and herbs, which contribute to its unique taste profile.

The history of Queso Payoyo is relatively recent compared to other traditional Spanish cheeses. It was developed in the 1990s by a group of local farmers and cheesemakers in the Sierra de Grazalema Natural Park. Their goal was to preserve and promote the indigenous livestock breeds and to create a high-quality cheese that could stand out in the competitive cheese market. The effort paid off, and in 2013, the Spanish Ministry of Agriculture awarded Queso Payoyo the title of Spain's Best Cheese. It also won a bronze medal at the World's Best Cheese awards in 2014.

For wine pairings, Queso Payoyo is best enjoyed with a glass of dry sherry, which complements its flavor and creamy texture. Alternatively, it pairs well with red wines such as Rioja or Tempranillo, which bring out its rich taste. Serving the cheese with crusty bread can also highlight its flavors and create a satisfying combination.

In Spanish cuisine, Queso Payoyo is often served as part of a cheese platter, accompanied by nuts, dried fruits, and honey. It can also be used in various dishes to add a rich flavor. One popular dish is a salad featuring Queso Payoyo, mixed greens, and a drizzle of olive oil and balsamic vinegar. The cheese's creamy texture and intense flavor make it a standout ingredient in many recipes. Additionally, it can be melted over grilled vegetables for a delicious and hearty meal.

41. Burrata di Andria

Italy | **Soft** | **Cow**

Burrata di Andria, made from cow's milk, specifically mozzarella and cream, is famously known as "the queen of cheeses." This Italian delicacy hails from Apulia, particularly the town of Andria. Although Burrata has been produced only since the 1950s, it has swiftly become an Italian classic. The outer shell is solid mozzarella, while the inside is a mix of mozzarella and cream, giving it a unique, soft texture.

Interestingly, Burrata was created as a way to reduce food waste by utilizing the leftovers from mozzarella production. This innovation turned into a celebrated delicacy. The cheese's name, "Burrata," comes from the Italian word for butter, highlighting its rich and creamy interior.

Burrata di Andria has a delicate yet rich flavor of fresh milk. It is most often served simply with salt, pepper, and a drizzle of extra virgin olive oil. This simplicity allows the natural flavors to shine. It also pairs beautifully with bruschettas topped with prosciutto, tomatoes, and various fresh vegetables, making it a versatile addition to many dishes.

For wine pairing, a crisp and refreshing white wine like Vermentino complements the creamy texture and mild flavor of Burrata. The acidity in the wine balances the richness of the cheese, creating a harmonious combination.

In local Apulian cuisine, Burrata is featured in several traditional dishes. One popular dish is "Orecchiette con Burrata," where the cheese is combined with the region's famous ear-shaped pasta, cherry tomatoes, and fresh basil. Another delightful preparation is "Burrata Caprese," a variation of the classic Caprese salad, where Burrata replaces the traditional mozzarella, paired with ripe tomatoes, fresh basil, and a drizzle of balsamic glaze.

40. Gołka

Poland | **Soft** | **Cow**

Gołka is a traditional smoked Polish cheese from the region of Silesia, made exclusively from cow's milk. This cheese is light yellow in color and has a unique cylindrical shape, achieved by placing it in carved wooden molds that also impart a decorative pattern on its rind. Gołka's delicate taste, smoky flavor, and soft texture make it a distinctive addition to any cheese board.

Historically, Gołka has been a part of Polish culinary traditions for many years, especially in Silesia, where dairy farming is prevalent. The method of smoking the cheese was initially developed as a means of preservation, allowing the cheese to last longer. This technique also imparted a distinct flavor that has become a signature characteristic of Gołka. The use of wooden molds is a nod to the traditional craftsmanship of the region, highlighting the cultural significance and artisanal nature of this cheese.

Gołka pairs exceptionally well with light to medium-bodied white wines, such as a dry Riesling or a crisp Picpoul de Pinet. The acidity and freshness of these wines complement the cheese's smoky notes and bring out its delicate flavor. Additionally, a fruity red wine like a Shiraz can also be a good match, providing a pleasing contrast to the cheese's soft texture and subtle taste. For an even richer experience, try serving Gołka with fresh fruits or nuts.

In Polish cuisine, Gołka is often enjoyed with fruit preserves and fresh bread, allowing the cheese's flavors to shine. It is also used in various dishes, such as "Gołka stuffed pierogi," where the cheese is combined with potatoes and herbs to create a rich and flavorful filling. Another popular dish is "Gołka and vegetable gratin," which layers slices of the cheese with seasonal vegetables and bakes them until bubbly and golden. The cheese's melt-in-your-mouth texture and smoky flavor add depth to these traditional recipes.

39. Njeguški Sir

Montenegro | **Hard** | **Sheep**

Njeguški sir is a traditional Montenegrin full-fat hard cheese made from sheep's milk. The production process starts by placing the curd in a cheesecloth, then into a cheese mold, and finally pressing it with a wooden plank topped with a stone. After one day, the cheese is salted and stored in a wooden box for two days. It is then left to mature for at least four weeks until it is ready for consumption.

The final product has a golden-yellow crust and a distinctive milky-sour, salty flavor. Njeguški sir originates from the village of Njeguši in Montenegro, a place known for its rich cheese-making traditions. The methods used to make Njeguški sir have been passed down through generations, reflecting the local culture and heritage. Historically, Njeguški sir was made by shepherds in the mountainous regions of Montenegro. The natural environment and traditional practices contributed to the unique flavor of the cheese. It was often made in small quantities, primarily for family consumption and local markets.

Njeguški sir pairs well with Montenegrin wines, particularly a dry white wine such as Krstač. The wine's acidity complements the cheese's salty and milky-sour notes, creating a balanced tasting experience. For those who prefer red wine, a light Vranac also pairs nicely, contributing to the cheese's rich flavors.

In Montenegrin cuisine, Njeguški sir is featured in several local dishes. One popular dish is "Njeguški steak," where the cheese is stuffed inside a pork or veal cutlet, then grilled to perfection. The cheese melts inside, adding a creamy and flavorful element to the meat. Another traditional dish is "Polenta with Njeguški sir," where the cheese is grated over hot polenta, allowing it to melt and blend with the creamy cornmeal. The cheese is also enjoyed simply with bread and olives, highlighting its natural flavors.

38. Manchego viejo

Spain | **Hard** | **Sheep**

Manchego viejo is a type of Manchego cheese, representing the fourth and final stage of aging. Made from sheep's milk, this cheese undergoes a maturation process lasting from one to two years in natural caves. The result is a firm, crumbly texture and a deep, rich yellow color.

The flavors of Manchego viejo are complex and deep, characterized by a sharp kick and a slightly peppery edge. This cheese has a rich history dating back to the Bronze Age, with evidence of sheep farming and cheese production in the La Mancha region. The traditional methods of making Manchego cheese have been preserved through generations, contributing to its distinctive taste and quality.

For wine pairings, Manchego viejo goes well with a bold red wine such as Tempranillo. The strong flavors of the wine complement the cheese's sharpness and complexity. A dry sherry is also a good match, as its nutty and slightly sweet notes balance the cheese's intense flavors. Additionally, a full-bodied white wine like Chardonnay can also pair nicely, offering a smooth contrast to the cheese's richness.

In Spanish cuisine, Manchego viejo is often used in a variety of dishes. One popular dish is "Manchego and Chorizo Tapas," where slices of the cheese are served alongside spicy chorizo sausage, creating a flavorful contrast. Another traditional dish is "Ensalada Manchega," a salad featuring crumbled Manchego viejo, tomatoes, olives, and a light vinaigrette. The cheese's firm texture and sharp taste add depth to the salad. Additionally, Manchego viejo is frequently grated over pasta dishes, allowing their flavor with its rich, nutty profile.

Manchego viejo can also be enjoyed on its own, served with crusty bread and a selection of nuts and dried fruits. This allows the cheese's full range of flavors to be appreciated.

37. Krasotyri

Greece | Soft | Sheep, Goat

Krasotyri is a traditional Greek cheese from the island of Kos. Made from sheep's or goat's milk, or sometimes a combination of both, this cheese undergoes a unique aging process that gives it its distinctive character. The milk is first warmed and pasteurized, then placed into containers and traditional elongated wicker molds for draining.

Once the cheese has formed, it is placed in brine to enhance its flavor and preservation. After brining, the cheese is combined with wine sediment and left to age for up to 20 days. This process infuses the cheese with a distinct wine flavor, setting it apart from other Greek cheeses. The texture of Krasotyri is delicate and soft, and its aroma is rich with wine notes.

Historically, the production of Krasotyri on Kos has deep roots, reflecting the island's long tradition of cheese-making and winemaking. The practice of using wine sediment in the aging process is a testament to the ingenuity of local cheesemakers, who found a way to combine two of the island's most important products—cheese and wine—into a single delicacy.

Krasotyri pairs excellently with Kefalonia wine. Kefalonia wines, such as those made from the local Robola grape, offer a crisp acidity and subtle citrus flavors that balance the cheese's richness and sharpness. The bright, refreshing qualities of the Kefalonia wine complement Krasotyri's bold taste without overwhelming it, making for a harmonious combination.

One popular way to enjoy Krasotyri is in "Krasotyri and Tomato Salad," where the cheese is crumbled over fresh tomatoes, cucumbers, and onions, then drizzled with olive oil and sprinkled with oregano. Another dish is "Stuffed Peppers with Krasotyri," where the cheese is mixed with rice, herbs, and spices, then stuffed into bell peppers and baked until tender.

36. Graviera Agrafon

Greece | **Hard** | **Goat, Sheep**

Graviera Agrafon is a delicious hard table cheese produced exclusively from sheep milk or a mixture of sheep milk and no more than 30% goat milk. This cheese has been crafted for over a century in the mountainous Agrafon area of the Karditsa prefecture, capturing the aroma and flavor of mountain herbs.

The cheese undergoes a ripening process for around three months, during which microflora develop on its surface, contributing to its maturation and characteristic scent. Graviera Agrafon is a hard, round cheese, typically available in sizes ranging from 2 to 3 kilos. Its interior is compact and dotted with small holes, giving it a unique texture. Despite not being as popular as Graviera Naxou or Graviera Kritis, this bright yellow cheese has a slightly sweet taste and rich aroma that make it a must-try for cheese enthusiasts. Its unique flavor profile is a testament to the traditional cheesemaking methods of the Agrafon region.

Graviera Agrafon has a rich history rooted in the pastoral traditions of the Agrafon mountains. The local shepherds have been perfecting their cheesemaking techniques for generations, ensuring that each wheel of Graviera Agrafon embodies the essence of the region's flora and fauna.

For a delightful wine pairing, Graviera Agrafon pairs well with tannic red wines. A robust Greek Xinomavro, with its complex structure and fruity notes, complements the cheese's slightly sweet and aromatic profile. Alternatively, a Cabernet Sauvignon with its bold tannins and dark fruit flavors also makes an excellent pairing.

In Greek cuisine, Graviera Agrafon is used in a variety of dishes. One famous recipe is "Saganaki," where the cheese is pan-fried until golden and crispy, creating a delectable appetizer. Another popular dish is "Graviera-stuffed Peppers," where the cheese is melted inside sweet bell peppers, offering a delightful blend of flavors.

35. Beaufort

France | **Hard** | **Cow**

Named after its town of origin and produced in the French Rhône-Alpes region since the Middle Ages, Beaufort is a hard cheese made from the raw milk of the Tarentaise cattle breed. This cheese is matured much longer than its softer Alpine counterparts, typically around four to five months. During the first two months, Beaufort is salt-rubbed on a daily basis. Once the rind has matured enough, the cheese wheels are smeared with morge—a mixture of brine, whey, and old cheese scrapings. This process contributes to its unique flavor and texture. Beaufort comes in three varieties: Le Beaufort, produced from November to May; Le Beaufort d'Été, produced in the summer; and Le Beaufort Chalet d'Alpage, the most prized variety made in Alpine chalets using milk from a single herd of cows pastured at altitudes of 1500 meters and above.

Historically, Beaufort has played a significant role in the local economy and culture of the Rhône-Alpes region. The use of milk from Tarentaise cattle, a breed adapted to the high-altitude pastures, contributes to the unique qualities of Beaufort.

Beaufort pairs excellently with white wine such as dry Savoy wine like Apremont, which complement its buttery and fruity flavors. For those who prefer red wine, a light Pinot Noir also works well, offering a delicate balance to the cheese's rich taste.

In French cuisine, Beaufort is used in various traditional dishes. One famous dish is "Fondue Savoyarde," a classic Alpine cheese fondue that combines Beaufort with other local cheeses, creating a creamy and flavorful dip for bread and vegetables. Another popular dish is "Tartiflette," a hearty gratin made with potatoes, onions, lardons, and slices of Beaufort, baked until golden and bubbly. Beaufort is also delicious in "Gratin Dauphinois," where it is layered with thinly sliced potatoes and cream, then baked to perfection.

34. Picodon

Picodon is a small, round cheese made from goat's milk, weighing at least 60 grams, and produced in the Ardèche and Drôme regions of France. The cheese has a thin rind, often displaying yellow or white mold speckled with blue on the exterior. The maturation period for Picodon is at least 14 days, although it can be aged longer for a more intense flavor.

On the inside, Picodon is white or yellow, with a fine texture that becomes crumbly as it matures. Initially, the flavor is fresh and clean, balancing salty and acidic notes. However, as the cheese ages and dries out, losing half of its mass, its flavor becomes more concentrated and sharp.

Historically, Picodon has been produced in these regions for centuries, with records dating back to the 14th century. The name "Picodon" comes from the Occitan word "pica," meaning sharp, referring to the cheese's distinctive taste. The traditional methods of making Picodon reflect the region's rich agricultural heritage, where goat farming and cheese-making have long been integral to local life.

Picodon pairs well with both red and dry white wines. A light red wine like Côtes du Rhône or a dry white such as Viognier complements the cheese's fresh and tangy flavors. The acidity in these wines balances the cheese's sharpness, creating a harmonious pairing.

In French cuisine, Picodon is often enjoyed after a meal, paired with garlic and shallots. It can also be featured in several local dishes. One popular preparation is "Picodon en Croûte," where the cheese is wrapped in puff pastry and baked until golden, served with a side salad. Another traditional dish is "Salade de Picodon," a salad with mixed greens, walnuts, and slices of Picodon, dressed with a light vinaigrette.

33. Oaxaca Cheese

Mexico		Semi-Soft		Cow

Oaxaca cheese, also known as Queso Oaxaca, is a semi-soft white cheese made from cow's milk, known for its distinctive stringy texture. It has a savory, creamy, mild, and buttery flavor, which makes it ideal for a variety of dishes such as quesadillas, empanadas, and tlayudas. The cheese's excellent melting properties also make it a popular choice for numerous baked dishes.

Named after the Oaxaca state in southern Mexico, Oaxaca cheese has an interesting historical background. The pasta filata cheesemaking process used to create Oaxaca cheese originates from Italy. It was brought to Mexico by Dominican friars who settled in Oaxaca. These friars adapted the traditional Italian methods to local ingredients and conditions, resulting in the creation of this unique Mexican cheese.

For pairing a crisp Mexican lager, such as Pacifico. The beer's light, refreshing taste and mild hop bitterness complement the creamy and mild flavor of Oaxaca cheese. Additionally, a Mexican white wine like Chenin Blanc from Baja California, with its bright acidity and notes of green apple, pear, and citrus, also pairs well, balancing the cheese's texture and flavor.

In Mexican cuisine, Oaxaca cheese is used in a variety of traditional dishes. One popular dish is the "Tlayuda", a large, crispy tortilla topped with refried beans, meats, and shredded Oaxaca cheese, then baked or grilled until the cheese melts. Another favorite is "Quesadillas", where the cheese is melted inside a folded tortilla, often with additional ingredients like mushrooms, squash blossoms, or chorizo. Oaxaca cheese is also used in chiles rellenos, where it is stuffed inside roasted poblano peppers and then fried. Oaxaca cheese can be enjoyed on its own, shredded over salads, or incorporated into casseroles and baked dishes. Its versatility and rich flavor make it a staple in many Mexican households and an essential ingredient in Mexican cuisine.

32. Anthotyro

Greece | **Semi-Hard** | **Goat, Sheep**

Anthotyro is a traditional Greek cheese made from a blend of goat's and sheep's milk. Its name, meaning "flowery cheese," reflects the strong aromas of wild herbs that characterize its flavor. There are two main varieties of Anthotyro: fresh (anthotyro fresco) and dry (anthotyro xero).

The fresh variety, anthotyro fresco, has a soft texture and a mild, creamy flavor. It is commonly enjoyed as a table cheese or used in pastries and pies. One popular way to enjoy anthotyro fresco is by pairing it with honey and fresh fruits like apples, pears, and figs. This combination highlights the cheese's delicate taste and creamy texture, making it a delightful addition to any meal.

The dry variety, anthotyro xero, has a rich, salty flavor and a crumbly texture. This version is often consumed as a table cheese or grated over dishes such as pasta and salads. Its flavor makes it a great topping for spaghetti, adding a savory touch to the dish. The cheese is made in various regions across Greece, each adding its local touch to the process. The fresh version is typically made during the spring and summer months when the milk is plentiful and rich in flavor due to the goats and sheep grazing on fresh herbs and grasses.

Pairing Anthotyro with wine depends on its variety. For the fresh anthotyro fresco, a light white wine such as Moschofilero complements its mild flavor and creamy texture. For the dry anthotyro xero, a fuller-bodied white wine like Assyrtiko or a light red wine such as Xinomavro works well, balancing its salty and rich taste.

Anthotyro is also featured in various Greek dishes. Fresh anthotyro is often used in Spanakopita, a savory spinach and cheese pie, and in desserts like cheesecake, where its mild flavor and creamy texture shine. Dry anthotyro is excellent in traditional Greek pasta dishes, grated over a plate of hot spaghetti with olive oil and herbs.

31. Bundz

Bundz also known as "bunc" in the Podhale dialect, is a traditional Polish cheese made from sheep's milk, produced primarily in the mountainous regions of the country. Its flavor and texture are reminiscent of cottage cheese, offering a mild, fresh taste.

Bundz is a cheese with roots in the Carpathian region of Poland and Ukraine. The production process of Bundz begins similarly to that of Oscypek (number 100). Fresh sheep's milk is poured into a container called "putara" and coagulated using rennet, an enzyme from the stomachs of young calves. The curds that form are then briefly heated to about 70 °C before being strained on canvas to form large lumps, resulting in a mild, soft cheese.

Bundz pairs well with wines that can balance its lightness. A crisp white wine such as Pouilly-Fumé or a dry Riesling works well, as their acidity and citrus notes complement the cheese's tanginess without overpowering it. For a red option, a light Californian Pinot Noir offers a subtle fruitiness that matches the cheese's delicate flavor. These wine choices help to bring out the best in Bundz, creating a balanced pairing that highlights both the cheese and the wine's characteristics.

In Polish cuisine, Bundz is often enjoyed in a variety of dishes. One popular preparation is "Bundz Salad," where the cheese is crumbled over a mix of fresh vegetables like tomatoes, cucumbers, and radishes, and dressed with a light vinaigrette. Another traditional dish is "Pierogi with Bundz," where the cheese is used as a filling for the famous Polish dumplings, often combined with potatoes and herbs for added flavor.

The leftover whey from Bundz production is used to make żętyca, a traditional sour beverage enjoyed in the mountainous regions. This drink highlights the resourcefulness of Polish cheesemakers, utilizing every part of the milk.

30. Salašnícky Údený Syr

Slovakia | **Soft** | **Sheep**

Ovčí salašnícky údený syr is a traditional Slovakian cheese made from unpasteurized sheep's milk. This soft cheese is handcrafted in the mountainous regions and shepherd's huts, known as salaš, which is reflected in its name. The cheese is known for its unique shapes, often formed into lumps, hearts, cockerels, or other animals.

The cheese-making process includes smoking the cheese over hardwood, which gives it a firm and dry exterior with a crust and small stains from the smoking. Inside, the cheese is yellow with a firm texture and small holes that develop when sliced. The flavor of Ovčí salašnícky údený syr is smoky, mild, delicate, and slightly acidic. Historically, smoking was used to extend the cheese's shelf life, allowing it to be consumed during winter when fresh cheese was not available.

The Slovakian dairy tradition is ancient and deeply rooted in the region. Over centuries, it has become a crucial means of subsistence for the inhabitants. In particular, sheep breeding has been refined in the mountainous areas to produce sheep's cheeses. The word "salasnícky" originates from "salas," meaning the shepherd's shelter where freshly milked sheep's milk was stored for processing. It has always been considered a delicacy, but since the 20th century, Ovčí Salašnícky Údený Syr TSG has gained fame throughout Slovakia and beyond its borders.

For wine pairing a great match is a white wine like Rizling Rýnsky (Riesling). Slovakian Riesling is known for its bright acidity, floral aromas, and notes of green apple, citrus, and minerality. The wine's acidity and freshness complement the smoky and tangy flavors of the cheese, while its minerality enhances the savory characteristics.

Ovčí Salašnícky Údený Syr TSG should be stored in the least cold compartment of the refrigerator. It makes a tasty snack on its own, and when paired with sausages and vegetables, it turns into a satisfying meal.

29. Redykołka

Poland | Semi-Hard | Sheep

Redykołka is a traditional Polish cheese from the Podhale region, made from half-fat sheep's milk. The name comes from "redyk," a term referring to the ceremonial practice of taking sheep to and from mountain pastures. Redykołka is a semi-hard cheese and is typically crafted into unique shapes such as small animals, birds, hearts, or spindles. The cheese pieces weigh no more than 300 grams, with the smallest spindle-shaped ones ranging from 30 to 60 grams.

The production of Redykołka involves using the leftovers from making Oscypek, (another famous Polish cheese, Number 95 on the list) . Because of their similarities, Redykołka is often mistaken for Oscypek. Traditionally, Redykołka was given as a gift by shepherds to children or guests, always in even numbers. This custom highlights its cultural significance and the cheese's role in social and festive occasions.

Redykołka has a smooth, white interior and a straw-colored exterior, a result of the smoking process. The flavor is slightly salty, smoky, and mildly spicy, making it a distinctive treat. Its small size and unique shapes make it visually appealing as well as flavorful.

When it comes to wine pairing, a medium-bodied red like a Cabernet Franc or a Merlot works well, as their fruitiness and moderate tannins complement the cheese's bold taste. For a white wine, a dry Riesling offers a crisp, refreshing contrast that cuts through the cheese's richness.

In Polish cuisine, Redykołka is enjoyed in various ways. It can be served as an appetizer, sliced and paired with fresh bread, or included in cheese platters. Redykołka is also used in salads, adding a smoky depth to the dish. Another popular way to enjoy this cheese is by melting it over grilled vegetables or incorporating it into traditional Polish dishes like pierogi.

28. Provolone del Monaco

Italy | **Semi-Hard** | **Cow**

Provolone del Monaco is a traditional Italian cheese produced since the 1700s by shepherds in the Lattari Mountains, which is the largest milk production area around Naples and Vico Equense. This melon-shaped, semi-hard cheese is made from raw cow's milk. The name "Provolone del Monaco" originates from the shepherds' long, hooded cowls, which led people to believe the cheese was produced by monks.

A key characteristic of Provolone del Monaco is that at least 20% of the milk used in its production comes from the endangered Agerolese dairy cattle breed. This contributes to the exceptional quality of its spun paste. The cheese has a sweet and buttery flavor with a pleasantly piquant aftertaste that becomes more pronounced as it ages.

Historically, Provolone del Monaco has been a staple in Neapolitan cuisine. Its origins in the Lattari Mountains, combined with the unique qualities of the Agerolese cattle, make it a cheese rich in tradition and flavor. The aging process enhances its distinctive taste, making it a versatile ingredient in many dishes.

Provolone del Monaco pairs well with aged red wines. A bold Chianti or a full-bodied Barolo complements the cheese's sweet and piquant flavors. The complexity of these wines balances the richness of the cheese, creating a harmonious pairing. Additionally, a rich Amarone can also be an excellent match.

In Italian cuisine, Provolone del Monaco is used in various traditional dishes. One popular dish is "Gnocchi alla Sorrentina," where the cheese is melted into a tomato sauce with gnocchi, creating a creamy and flavorful dish. Another one is "Melanzane alla Parmigiana," an eggplant parmesan where Provolone del Monaco adds depth and richness to the layers of eggplant, tomato sauce, and basil. The cheese is also excellent as a table cheese, served with fresh bread, olives, and a drizzle of olive oil.

27. Miročki sir

Miročki sir is a traditional Serbian cheese, known for its fresh, full-fat composition primarily made from cow's milk, though sheep's and goat's milk can also be included. This cheese has a semi-hard texture and a slightly sweet flavor. The production process involves briefly cooking the cheese in its own whey, followed by salting and leaving it in brine for two days.

The history of Miročki sir is deeply rooted in the region of eastern Serbia, particularly in the Miroč mountain area. This cheese has been a local delicacy for centuries, enjoyed by shepherds and villagers alike. Traditionally, fresh Miročki cheese was treated as a special treat, often skewered and grilled over open flames. When grilled, the cheese develops a crunchy exterior while the interior stays soft but not melted, providing a delightful contrast in textures.

Miročki sir pairs wonderfully with various foods and wines. Due to its fatty and intense flavor, it is best complemented by cherry tomatoes, figs, pomegranate, and honey. These accompaniments balance the cheese's richness and enhance its slightly sweet undertones. For wine pairing, A perfect match is with Prokupac, a native Serbian red wine. Prokupac is known for its medium body, bright acidity, and flavors of red berries, cherries, and subtle earthy notes. The wine's acidity and fruitiness complement the tangy and nutty characteristics of Miročki sir, while its medium body balances the cheese's semi-hard texture.

Marinating the cheese in orange juice before grilling can add a subtle citrus note that pairs well with the cheese's natural sweetness. This method brings out the best in the cheese and is highly recommended for those looking to experience its traditional preparation. Additionally, this marination technique can make the cheese more tender and flavorful, providing a unique twist to its taste.

26. Kefalograviera

Greece | **Hard** | **Sheep, Goat**

Kefalograviera is one of the most renowned Greek cheeses, known for its firm texture and light brown rind. Made primarily from sheep's milk or a combination of sheep's and goat's milk, it has a distinctive taste that blends the salty, intense flavors of Kefalotyri with the mellow notes of Graviera. This hard table cheese has been produced since the 1960s in regions like Western Macedonia, Epirus, Aitoloakarnania, Evrytania, and western mainland Greece, making it a relatively new addition to the Greek cheese market. Kefalograviera is sold in wheels or wedges and is easily recognized by its firm texture and light brown rind. Its popularity has been on the rise, with an annual production of around 3,000 tons, making it one of the most widespread cheeses in Greece.

The history of Kefalograviera is rooted in the adaptation and blending of traditional Greek cheese-making techniques. By combining elements of Kefalotyri and Graviera, cheesemakers have created a product that captures the best characteristics of both cheeses. This approach has contributed to Kefalograviera's unique place in Greek cuisine.

Kefalograviera is often used in the preparation of saganaki, a popular Greek dish where the cheese is fried until it develops a golden crust. Its ability to withstand high heat without melting makes it ideal for this purpose. The cheese is also grated over pasta dishes, adding rich, salty flavor.

When it comes to wine pairings, Kefalograviera goes well with both red and white wines. A crisp white wine like Assyrtiko complements its salty flavors, while a light red wine such as Agiorgitiko pairs nicely with its rich taste. Additionally, pairing it with a Malagousia, another Greek white wine, can bring out the cheese's savory notes. For a traditional Greek experience, serve Kefalograviera with olives and fresh bread.

25. West Country Cheddar

England | **Semi-Hard** | **Cow**

West Country Farmhouse Cheddar is a unique type of Cheddar cheese known for its maturity, distinctive full flavor, and the traditional handmade methods used in its production. This cheese hails from the four counties of Dorset, Somerset, Devon, and Cornwall in England. Unlike mass-produced Cheddar, West Country Farmhouse Cheddar is made using milk from local farms and needs to mature for at least 9 months before it is ready for sale. It can be found in both cylindrical shapes and blocks of various sizes. The flavor of West Country Farmhouse Cheddar is full, sharp, and nutty, making it a favorite among cheese connoisseurs. Inside, the cheese is firm and creamy yellow with a crumbly texture. Its rich taste is a result of the traditional methods of production that have been passed down through generations.

Historically, Cheddar cheese originated in the village of Cheddar in Somerset, England, during the 12th century. The unique process known as "cheddaring," which involves stacking and turning the curds to expel whey, was developed here. West Country Farmhouse Cheddar continues to be made using these age-old techniques, ensuring its distinctive taste and quality.

For West Country Farmhouse Cheddar, a classic pairing includes both red and white wines. A Cabernet Sauvignon is a great choice, as its deep flavors and tannins complement the cheese's sharpness and nutty profile. On the white wine side, a fruity Zinfandel can also pair nicely with the cheddar, offering a slightly spicier contrast that highlights the cheese's complex flavors.

In local cuisine, West Country Farmhouse Cheddar is used in a variety of dishes. One popular dish is "Cheddar Ploughman's Lunch," which includes thick slices of the cheese served with crusty bread, pickles, and cold meats. Another favorite is "Cheddar and Leek Tart," where the cheese is combined with sautéed leeks in a savory pastry. The cheese is also perfect for grating over baked potatoes or adding to a cheese sauces,.

24. Stracciata

Stracciata is an artisan Italian cheese from the Molise region, made from cow's milk. The production process involves cutting or tearing the curd and then stretching it into ribbons that can be folded or braided. While stracciata is typically snow-white, it can develop a yellowish hue during the spring and summer months. The cheese's name comes from the Italian verb "stracciare," meaning to tear, reflecting the method used to create its unique texture.

On the outside, stracciata is buttery, mild, sweet, fresh, and slightly salty. The inside is milky and piquant, and the cheese melts in the mouth, leaving notes of warm melted butter on the palate. Historically, stracciata has been a staple in the Molise region, where local cheesemakers have perfected this delicate process over generations. The cheese's production method and its seasonal variations highlight the traditional and artisanal nature of Molise's dairy practices.

Stracciata pairs well with a crisp, refreshing white wine such as Pinot Grigio, which complements its mild and creamy flavors. Alternatively, a light and fruity red wine like Barbera can also pair nicely, adding a subtle contrast to the cheese's buttery notes.

In Italian cuisine, stracciata is enjoyed in various ways. One popular local dish is "Stracciata with Prosciutto and Arugula," where the cheese is paired with thin slices of prosciutto, fresh arugula, and a drizzle of olive oil, served on crusty bread. Another traditional dish is "Stracciata Salad," which combines the cheese with ripe tomatoes, basil, and a balsamic vinaigrette, creating a fresh and flavorful salad.

Stracciata is also excellent as a topping for pizza, where it melts beautifully, or as a filling for stuffed pasta dishes like ravioli, adding a creamy texture and rich flavor.

23. Délice de Bourgogne

France | **Soft** | **Cow**

Délice de Bourgogne is a French triple crème cheese from the Burgundy region, made from cow's milk and enriched with butterfat, resulting in a fat content of 75%. This cheese boasts a smooth, creamy texture and a rich flavor profile that includes tangy, tart, salty, buttery, and mushroomy notes. The rind is white, bloomy, and carries a pungent aroma.

Historically, Délice de Bourgogne was created in the 1970s by Jean Lincet in the Burgundy region, a place known for its rich culinary traditions and exceptional cheeses. The addition of extra cream to the cheese during production elevates its creaminess and flavor, making it a standout among triple crème cheeses. This tradition of enhancing cheese with extra cream dates back to the early cheese-making practices in Burgundy, where local cheesemakers aimed to create products with distinct textures and flavors.

Délice de Bourgogne pairs wonderfully with ciders and white wines. A crisp, dry Champagne or a Chardonnay from Burgundy complements the cheese's buttery and tangy flavors perfectly. The acidity and bubbles in Champagne help to cut through the richness of the cheese, creating a balanced tasting experience. In terms of cider, Délice de Bourgogne pairs beautifully with a Normandy cider. The apple-forward flavors and crisp acidity of the cider contrast nicely with the cheese's richness, cutting through its creaminess and offering a refreshing balance.

In terms of local dishes, Délice de Bourgogne can be used in several delicious ways. One popular dish is "Délice de Bourgogne Tart," where the cheese is spread over a flaky pastry crust and topped with caramelized onions and fresh herbs, then baked until golden and bubbly. Another local favorite is "Gratin Dauphinois," where slices of Délice de Bourgogne are layered with thinly sliced potatoes and cream, creating a decadent and creamy gratin.

22. Canastra

Brazil | **Semi-Hard** | **Cow**

Canastra is a Brazilian cheese made from raw cow's milk, originating from the Serra da Canastra region in the state of Minas Gerais. Named after its place of origin, Canastra is a cylindrical cheese that can be either semi-hard or slightly softer, with a mildly acidic and slightly spicy flavor.

The traditional maturation period for Canastra is 21 days, but some producers extend this up to 40 days. When matured longer, the cheese develops a flavor reminiscent of Grana Padano. Historically, Canastra was made for special occasions, such as visits from royalty and captains, showcasing its cultural importance. In 2008, it was declared an intangible cultural heritage of Brazil, highlighting its significance in Brazilian culinary traditions.

Canastra pairs well with red wine, such as a rich, full-bodied Cabernet Sauvignon or a smooth, velvety Merlot, both of which complement its mildly acidic and spicy notes. A dark beer, like a robust stout or porter, also makes a great pairing, as its deep flavors balance the cheese's unique taste. Additionally, serving Canastra with guava paste (goiabada) creates a delightful contrast between the cheese's sharpness and the sweetness of the paste. This combination brings out the best in both the cheese and the guava paste, making it a popular choice for cheese boards.

In Brazilian cuisine, Canastra is enjoyed in various ways. One popular dish is "Pão de Queijo," where grated Canastra is mixed into the dough of these famous cheese breads, giving them a rich flavor. Another traditional dish is "Tutu de Feijão," a thick bean stew where Canastra is crumbled on top, adding a creamy texture and enhancing the dish's flavors. The cheese is also excellent when served simply with fresh bread and fruit, allowing its natural taste to shine.

21. Comté

France | **Semi-Hard** | **Cow**

Comté is a large, hard cheese made from unpasteurized cow's milk, containing at least 45% fat and characterized by a pressed, cooked paste. This cheese, produced in the Jura massif in the Doubs, Jura, and Haute-Saône departments of France, offers a unique flavor profile that can vary from milky, spicy, and roasted to fruity, buttery, and plant-like. This diversity in taste is due to the immediate use of the milk after milking, which captures the fresh essence of the region's pastures.

Comté has been produced since the 12th century, making it one of France's oldest cheeses. Its production process has remained largely unchanged over the centuries, maintaining traditional methods. Each cheese wheel is aged for at least 120 days, during which it is turned and scrubbed regularly. Comté also carries a seasonal stamp, such as winter, summer, mountain Comté, or plains Comté, reflecting the time of year and location of production. This adds another layer of complexity and variation to its flavor.

The texture of Comté is creamy, making it versatile in its culinary uses. It can be sliced, grated, or cubed and melts easily, making it a popular choice for fondues. One traditional dish that highlights Comté is "Fondue Savoyarde," a classic Alpine cheese fondue where Comté is combined with other local cheeses. Another popular use is in "Gratin Dauphinois," where Comté is grated over thinly sliced potatoes and baked with cream to create a rich, golden crust.

Comté pairs exceptionally well with sherry and a variety of red wines. A light to medium-bodied Pinot Noir complements Comté's complexity without overpowering it, while a bolder red like Cabernet Sauvignon can bring out its spicier notes. Additionally, a dry white wine such as German Riesling can balance the richness of the cheese. For those who enjoy sparkling wines, a Brut Champagne can also be an excellent match, adding a refreshing contrast to the cheese's flavors.

20. Pecorino Toscano

Italy | **Semi-Hard** | **Sheep**

Pecorino Toscano, an Italian cheese, dates back to the 15th century when its production began in spring. At that time, it was called Cacio Marzolino, meaning "March cheese." Today, Pecorino Toscano is produced year-round in Tuscany and also in the neighboring regions of Lazio and Umbria. It is available in two forms: Fresco (fresh) and Stagionato (matured for at least 4 months).

This cheese is made with whole sheep's milk from animals grazing on pastures nestled between the Apennines and the Tyrrhenian Sea. Compared to other Pecorino varieties, Pecorino Toscano is only briefly salted, which helps it retain a delicate, sweet flavor.

For wine pairings, Pecorino Toscano pairs wonderfully with a variety of wines. A Chianti, with its bright acidity and cherry notes, complements the sweet and nutty flavors of the cheese. Alternatively, a crisp Vernaccia di San Gimignano also works well, balancing the cheese's creamy texture and slight saltiness. This combination brings out the best in both the wine and the cheese, making for a truly enjoyable experience. Pecorino Toscano can also be enjoyed with fresh fruit, which highlights its subtle sweetness.

In Tuscan cuisine, Pecorino Toscano is used in a variety of dishes. One popular dish is "Ribollita," a hearty Tuscan potage soup made with bread, vegetables, and beans, where grated Pecorino Toscano Stagionato adds depth and richness. Another favorite is "Pasta con Pecorino e Pepe," a simple pasta dish featuring freshly grated Pecorino Toscano and black pepper, showcasing the cheese's flavor. The cheese is also excellent served with fresh vegetables, fruits, jam, and honey, making it a versatile addition to any cheese platter.

19. Queijo de Azeitão

Portugal | **Semi-Soft** | **Sheep**

Queijo de Azeitão is a semi-soft cheese made from unpasteurized sheep's milk. The origins of this cheese date back to the 19th century when Gaspar Henriques de Paiva emigrated to the town of Azeitão. Out of nostalgia for his birthplace, he imported black dairy sheep from his hometown to Azeitão and brought cheesemakers from Beira Baixa to craft cheeses. De Paiva's Azeitão cheeses quickly gained fame throughout Portugal, winning several awards at agricultural fairs.

The milk for Queijo de Azeitão comes from sheep that graze on natural vegetation in the pastures of Azeitão. These sheep are milked manually, and the milk is mixed with the extract of a local variety of thistle to start the curdling process, making the cheese 100% vegetarian. Salt is added to the curd, which is then manually worked and wrapped into muslin cloth bundles, known as cinchos. The finished cheese is round and flat with a yellowish crust, concealing a light-colored interior with a semi-solid consistency. The flavor of Queijo de Azeitão is both sour and salty, with herby undertones. This runny cheese is best enjoyed scooped onto a slice of fresh bread. It also makes a delightful dessert when paired with fruit and a semi-dry white wine.

For wine pairings, Queijo de Azeitão pairs well with a semi-dry white wine like Vinho Verde. The light and slightly effervescent nature of Vinho Verde complements the cheese's sour and salty flavors, participating to its overall taste.

In Portuguese cuisine, Queijo de Azeitão is often enjoyed in various dishes. One popular way to serve it is as a starter, scooped onto slices of crusty bread with a drizzle of olive oil. Another local dish is "Salada de Queijo de Azeitão," where the cheese is crumbled over a fresh salad with tomatoes, olives, and mixed greens, dressed with a simple vinaigrette. It is also common to find this cheese paired with fresh fruit, such as apples or pears, offering a delightful contrast between the sweet fruit and the savory cheese.

18. Pecorino Sardo

Pecorino Sardo is a semi-cooked, hard cheese produced exclusively on the island of Sardinia. Made from whole milk of the pasture-grazing Sarda sheep, this cheese benefits from the unique flora of the Mediterranean region. The Sarda sheep, indigenous to Sardinia, are known for their high-quality milk production, which is essential to the cheese's distinctive flavor. These sheep graze on fragrant Mediterranean shrubs, imparting an aromatic quality to the cheese. Pecorino Sardo comes in two varieties: Pecorino Sardo Dolce (mild) and Pecorino Sardo Maturo (mature). The Dolce version is sweet and delicate, while the Maturo version is aged for at least two months, developing a stronger and pleasantly piquant flavor.

Historically, Pecorino Sardo has been a staple in Sardinian cuisine for centuries. The local shepherds have long relied on the adaptability of the Sarda sheep to the island's diverse terrains, ensuring a consistent supply of high-quality milk.

For wine pairings, Pecorino Sardo pairs well with both red and white wines. A Vermentino di Sardegna, a crisp and slightly fruity white wine, complements the mild and sweet flavors of Pecorino Sardo Dolce. For the more mature and robust Pecorino Sardo Maturo, a Cannonau, a full-bodied red wine from Sardinia, is an excellent choice. The wine's richness balances the cheese's strong and piquant notes.

In Sardinian cuisine, Pecorino Sardo is featured in a variety of dishes. Pecorino Sardo Dolce is often enjoyed as a table cheese, paired with fresh vegetables, grapes, or pears. It is also used in salads, adding a mild, creamy flavor. Pecorino Sardo Maturo, on the other hand, is typically grated over pasta dishes like "Malloreddus alla Campidanese," a traditional Sardinian pasta dish with sausage and tomato sauce. The mature cheese is also enjoyed at the end of a meal, served with bread, olive oil, and pine nuts.

17. Brillat-Savarin

France | Soft | Cow

Brillat-Savarin is a luxurious triple-cream cheese originally known by names like Excelsior, Délice des Gourmets, or Le Magnum. It was first produced in the late 1800s near Forges-les-Eaux in Normandy. In the 1930s, the cheese was renamed to honor Jean Anthelme Brillat-Savarin, an 18th-century gourmet, by the renowned French cheesemaker Henri Androuët. Today, Brillat-Savarin is produced year-round in both Normandy and Burgundy.

This soft, white-crusted cow's milk cheese boasts a minimum of 75% butterfat, encased in an edible, snowy rind. When fresh, Brillat-Savarin is luscious, creamy, and has a neutral to faintly sour taste. As it ages, the cheese develops more pronounced earthy flavors, making it a versatile addition to any cheese board.

Historically, the creation and naming of Brillat-Savarin reflect the rich culinary traditions of France, particularly the appreciation for gourmet foods and the legacy of Jean Anthelme Brillat-Savarin, who was a famed lawyer and politician known for his work, "The Physiology of Taste."

For wine pairings, Brillat-Savarin is best enjoyed with sparkling wines, which complement its rich and creamy texture. A classic Champagne or a sparkling wine such as Crémant de Bourgogne pairs beautifully with this cheese, cutting through its richness with refreshing acidity.

Two popular French dishes made with Brillat-Savarin cheese are Tartines and Stuffed Chicken Breast. Tartines feature crusty baguette slices topped with the creamy cheese and various toppings like honey and caramelized onions, then lightly toasted. The stuffed chicken breast involves filling chicken with Brillat-Savarin and herbs, searing until golden, and finishing in the oven, resulting in a juicy, flavorful dish often served with roasted vegetables or a light salad.

16. Kalathaki Limnou

Greece | **Soft** | **Sheep, Goat**

Kalathaki Limnou is a white, soft, brined cheese made from fresh sheep's milk or a combination of sheep and goat milk. The animals graze freely on wild grasses on the island of Lemnos in the northern Aegean Sea. The production method of Kalathaki Limnou is similar to that of traditional feta cheese, with one significant difference that gives the cheese its name. The curd is placed in a kalathaki ("small basket") for draining and organic acidification, which imparts its characteristic cylindrical shape. After this process, the baskets are submerged in brine to mature for at least two months.

Historically, cheese-making on the island of Lemnos has been an essential part of local agriculture and diet for centuries. The traditional use of kalathaki baskets for shaping and draining the cheese is a practice that has been handed down through generations, reflecting the island's rich cultural heritage. This method not only shapes the cheese but also contributes to its unique texture and flavor profile.

For a wine pairing white wine like Malagousia, known for its aromatic profile with notes of peach, citrus, and herbs, has a balanced acidity that complements the cheese's tangy and salty characteristics. The wine's fruity and floral notes provide a refreshing contrast to the savory flavors of Kalathaki Limnou.

In Greek cuisine, Kalathaki Limnou is used in a variety of traditional dishes. One popular way to enjoy this cheese is in a classic Greek salad, where its mild flavor balances the tanginess of the tomatoes and the bitterness of the olives. Another delicious dish is "Spanakopita," a spinach pie where Kalathaki Limnou can be used as a substitute for feta, adding a unique twist to the traditional recipe. Additionally, Kalathaki Limnou can be used as a table cheese, served with fresh fruits like figs and grapes, or as a substitute cheese for saganaki, a dish where the cheese is fried until golden and served with lemon.

15. Pecorino Romano

Italy | **Hard** | **Sheep**

Pecorino Romano is a hard, cooked cheese made from whole milk of pasture-grazed sheep. Known for its salty and slightly piquant flavor, this cheese is aged for at least five months. It can be enjoyed as a table cheese, especially when paired with fresh vegetables and fruit. When aged for eight months or more, Pecorino Romano is typically grated over classic Roman dishes such as Bucatini all'Amatriciana, Rigatoni alla Carbonara, Spaghetti Cacio e Pepe, and Tripe alla Romana.

The origins of Pecorino Romano date back to the Roman Empire, with cheese processing methods documented by ancient Rome's prominent agricultural writers, including Varrone, Columella, Virgilio, and Pliny the Elder. By 227 BCE, the production of Pecorino Romano had spread to the neighboring island of Sardinia. Today, nearly 90% of Pecorino Romano is produced in Sardinia, with the remaining 10% coming from Lazio and the Tuscan province of Grosseto.

For wine pairings, Pecorino Romano goes well with a bold red wine like Chianti, which complements the cheese's strong, salty flavor. Alternatively, a crisp white wine such as Vermentino can balance the cheese's sharp notes, offering a refreshing contrast.

In Italian cuisine, Pecorino Romano is used in a variety of traditional dishes. One of the most iconic is Spaghetti Cacio e Pepe, where the cheese is grated over pasta with black pepper, creating a creamy and flavorful sauce. Another classic dish is Bucatini all'Amatriciana, a hearty pasta dish with tomato sauce, guanciale (cured pork cheek), and grated Pecorino Romano. Rigatoni alla Carbonara also showcases this cheese, blending it with eggs, pancetta, and black pepper to form a rich, velvety sauce. Additionally, Pecorino Romano is often sprinkled over Tripe alla Romana, boosting the dish's savory flavors.

14. Grana Padano

Italy | **Hard** | **Cow**

First produced in the 11th century by the Cistercian monks of the Santa Maria di Rovegnano Abbey in Chiaravalle Milanese, Grana Padano is one of the few parmesan cheeses that rivals the more famous Parmigiano-Reggiano. This hard cheese is made from unpasteurized, semi-skimmed cow's milk and comes in several varieties: Grana Padano, Trentin Grana, and Grana Grattugiato. It is sold at different ripening stages: Grana Padano (9-16 months), Grana Padano Oltre 16 mesi (over 16 months), and Grana Padano Riserva (over 20 months).

Today, Grana Padano is produced throughout the Po Valley, particularly in Lombardy, Trentino-Alto Adige, Veneto, and Emilia Romagna. As the cheese ages, its flavors become more pronounced, savory, and complex, while the texture becomes grainier and crumblier. The cheese's production and quality are overseen by the Consorzio di Tutela del Formaggio Grana Padano DOP, established in 1954. This organization ensures that only the highest quality cheeses pass the tests for aroma, appearance, and texture, protecting the cheese from imitations and promoting it globally.

Grana Padano can be enjoyed as a table cheese or grated over a wide array of dishes. Younger versions are typically paired with white wines such as Pinot Grigio, while Grana Padano Riserva pairs well with full-bodied red wines such as Barolo or Chianti. For food pairings, Grana Padano aged 9-16 months pairs nicely with apricots and black tea. Grana Padano Oltre 16 mesi goes well with strawberries and pepper, and the Riserva variety is exceptional with pears and Madagascar vanilla.

In Italian cuisine, Grana Padano is used in a variety of dishes. One popular dish is "Risotto alla Milanese," where the cheese is stirred into the risotto for a creamy texture and rich flavor. Another favorite is "Pasta alla Gricia," a traditional Roman pasta dish where grated Grana Padano enhances the dish's savory profile. The cheese is also perfect for grating over salads, soups, and vegetable dishes, adding depth.

13. Mont d'Or

France		Soft		Cow

Mont d'Or, also known as Vacherin du Haut-Doubs, is a soft cheese made from raw cow's milk in the Haut-Doubs region of France. One of the unique features of Mont d'Or is its presentation: it is encircled by spruce bark strips and packaged in a spruce wooden box, which helps maintain the cheese's shape.

The cheese offers a full, rich, sweet, and grassy flavor with a slightly acidic taste. Unlike most French cheeses, Mont d'Or's rind is not edible, so it must be removed to access the creamy, runny, almost liquid interior when fully ripe. This makes Mont d'Or ideal for eating like a fondue.

Historically, Mont d'Or has been produced in the Jura region since at least the 19th century. The method of encircling the cheese with spruce bark and packaging it in wooden boxes originated from local practices aimed at stabilizing the cheese during transportation and aging. These traditions have been passed down through generations, preserving the unique characteristics of Mont d'Or.

For wine pairings, Mont d'Or goes exceptionally well with sparkling wines such as Champagne or Crémant du Jura. The bubbles and acidity of the sparkling wine cut through the rich, creamy texture of the cheese, creating a balanced and enjoyable pairing.

In French cuisine, Mont d'Or is often served warm and enjoyed as a fondue. One popular dish is "Mont d'Or au Four," where the cheese is baked in its wooden box until melted and bubbly. It is typically served with boiled potatoes, charcuterie, and crusty bread for dipping. Another traditional preparation is "Mont d'Or avec des Pommes de Terre," a simple dish where the melted cheese is poured over baked or boiled potatoes, creating a comforting and delicious meal.

12. Reblochon

France | **Semi-Hard** | **Cow**

Reblochon is a semi-hard, pressed cheese weighing about 500 grams, made from unpasteurized cow's milk. It must ripen for at least 15 days in the Savoie and Haute-Savoie departments of France. According to an old tale, Reblochon originated because a farmer made the cheese to hide part of his milk production to lower the "milk taxes" paid to the pasture's owners.

Reblochon has a yellow to orange rind with an ivory body inside. The rind is edible, and the cheese has a nutty and slightly fruity taste. Its intense aroma is reminiscent of the cellars in which it matures. The cheese melts well and is excellent on baked potatoes.

Historically, Reblochon has been produced in the mountainous regions of Savoie and Haute-Savoie for centuries. The name "Reblochon" comes from the French word "reblocher," meaning "to pinch the cow's udder again." This refers to the practice of milking the cows a second time to obtain richer milk, which is used to make this cheese. This tradition has been maintained through generations, preserving the unique qualities of Reblochon.

For wine pairings, Reblochon goes well with a white wine from the same region, such as a Savoie Apremont or a Roussette de Savoie. These wines' crisp acidity and subtle fruitiness complement the cheese's nutty and slightly fruity flavors. Alternatively, a light red wine like Beaujolais can also pair nicely, balancing the cheese's rich taste.

In French cuisine, Reblochon is a key ingredient in several traditional dishes. One of the most famous is "Tartiflette," a hearty dish made with sliced potatoes, onions, lardons (bacon), and Reblochon cheese, all baked together until golden and bubbly. Another popular preparation is "Reblochon Fondue," where the cheese is melted and served with bread, boiled potatoes, and charcuterie for dipping. The cheese is also delicious when simply served with fresh bread and a salad.

11. Graviera Kritis

Greece | **Hard** | **Sheep, Goat**

Graviera Kritis is the best-known Greek Graviera cheese, with a long and storied history. This hard table cheese is produced using traditional methods in the prefectures of Hania, Rethymnos, Iraklion, and Lasithi on the island of Crete. It is typically made from sheep's milk or a mixture of sheep's milk with up to 20% goat's milk. The free-ranging sheep and goats graze on the island's diverse and aromatic flora, imparting a unique quality to their milk, which is then reflected in the cheese.

This hard table cheese is light yellow in color with a firm texture. Its taste is slightly sweet and nutty, developing through a maturation process of 3 to 5 months. This period allows the cheese to acquire its distinct flavor and texture, making it a favorite in Greek cuisine. Graviera Kritis is one of the most popular Greek cheeses, second only to feta, and it is widely available both within and outside Greece.

For wine pairings, Graviera Kritis goes well with both red and white wines. A fruity Moschofilero, with its aromatic and floral notes, complements the cheese's slight sweetness and nuttiness, making it an excellent choice for those who enjoy fragrant wines. Alternatively, a light red wine like Gamay can also be a good match, balancing the cheese's flavors without overpowering them.

In Greek cuisine, Graviera Kritis is used in a variety of dishes. It is often served as an appetizer, sliced and accompanied by olives and bread. The cheese is also grated over salads and soups, adding depth and flavor. One popular dish is "Saganaki," where Graviera Kritis is pan-fried until golden and served with a squeeze of lemon. Another traditional use is in "Dakos," a Cretan salad made with barley rusks, tomatoes, and a generous topping of grated Graviera Kritis.

10. Saint-Félicien

France | **Soft** | **Cow**

Saint-Félicien is a cow's milk cheese produced in the Rhône-Alpes region of France. It is designated as a dauphinois cheese, referring to the former French province of Dauphiné where it originated. This cheese is a close cousin of Saint-Marcellin, sharing a similar texture and taste, though Saint-Félicien can be almost twice as large in diameter. The name of the cheese comes from the small town of Saint-Félicien, where it was first produced and sold.

Originally, Saint-Félicien was made from goat's milk, but today it is more commonly produced with cow's milk. The cheese has a creamy interior encased in a flower-style (fleurie) rind. Each cheese typically weighs around 180 grams (6.3 oz). The optimal period for flavor is between April and September, after an aging period of 4 to 6 weeks, but it is also excellent when consumed between March and December. Saint-Félicien is softer and creamier than Saint-Marcellin, making it a luxurious treat for cheese lovers.

Saint-Félicien pairs beautifully with a variety of wines. A white wine such as a Viognier, with its floral and fruity notes, complements the cheese's creamy texture and subtle flavors. Alternatively, a light red wine like Beaujolais can also be a good match, balancing the cheese's richness without overwhelming it. This pairing allows the delicate qualities of the cheese to shine through, making for an enjoyable tasting experience.

In French cuisine, Saint-Félicien is often enjoyed on its own with fresh bread. It is also used in various dishes to add a creamy, rich element. One popular dish is "Gratin Dauphinois," a classic French gratin of potatoes, cream, and cheese, where Saint-Félicien adds a luxurious creaminess. Another traditional preparation is "Tarte aux Saint-Félicien," a savory tart made with a base of puff pastry, topped with caramelized onions and slices of the cheese, then baked until golden and bubbly.

9. Saint-André

Saint-André, often referred to as the "heavenly cheese," is a French triple-crème cheese made from cow's milk. It originated in Coutances in the Normandy region. Beneath its bloomy, edible rind lies a dense, creamy-textured body with mild and rich aromas. The flavors of Saint-André can be best described as sour, buttery, and slightly salty, with a tangy finish.

Historically, Saint-André was developed as an indulgent cheese to cater to those who enjoy the richness of creamier varieties. The addition of heavy cream during its production enhances its fat content to around 75%, making it one of the richest cheeses available. This luxurious texture and taste have made Saint-André a popular choice among cheese enthusiasts.

For wine pairings, Saint-André goes exceptionally well with a light and fruity rosé, which complements its creamy and tangy flavors. The wine's acidity balances the richness of the cheese, creating a harmonious pairing. Alternatively, a crisp Champagne can also enhance the buttery notes of Saint-André.

In French cuisine, Saint-André is often enjoyed in a variety of ways. One popular dish is Saint-André with Honey and Nuts, where the cheese is served with a drizzle of honey and a sprinkle of walnuts or almonds, creating a delightful contrast of flavors and textures. Another traditional preparation is "Saint-André Crostini," where slices of the cheese are spread on crusty bread and topped with pear slices and a touch of honey or balsamic glaze. The cheese also pairs wonderfully with fresh fruits like grapes, apples, and figs, making it a versatile addition to any cheese platter.

Saint-André can also be used in cooking to add richness to dishes. It melts beautifully and can be incorporated into creamy sauces for pasta or used as a decadent topping for baked potatoes.

Crottin de Chavignol

France | **Semi-Hard** | **Goat**

Crottin de Chavignol is a small, traditional French cheese made from raw goat's milk, weighing at least 60 grams. Its color ranges from white to ivory, and it features a dense, moist texture with a thin, moldy rind on the outside. The flavor of Crottin de Chavignol is full, slightly nutty, and distinctly "goaty," capturing the essence of its raw milk origins.

Historically, Crottin de Chavignol has been produced in the village of Chavignol in the Loire Valley for centuries. The name "crottin" comes from the French word for horse dung, which humorously describes the cheese's appearance as it ages. When young, the cheese is moist and creamy, but as it matures, it becomes drier and crumbly with a much harder rind that changes color dramatically, often darkening with age.

For wine pairings, young Crottin de Chavignol pairs beautifully with local white wines like Sancerre or Pouilly-Fumé. The crisp acidity and citrus notes of these wines complement the cheese's fresh, nutty flavors. Older, more mature Crottin de Chavignol pairs well with full-bodied Pinot Noir, such as Gevrey-Chambertin or Nuits-Saint-Georges. These wines are known for their depth, complexity, and rich flavors.

Two popular French dishes made with Crottin de Chavignol cheese are Salade de Chèvre Chaud and Tarte aux Crottin de Chavignol. Salade de Chèvre Chaud features rounds of Crottin de Chavignol that are lightly toasted or grilled until warm and slightly melted, then placed on a bed of mixed greens with walnuts, cherry tomatoes, and a light vinaigrette, creating a harmonious blend of flavors and textures. Tarte aux Crottin de Chavignol is a savory tart with a flaky pastry crust filled with a mixture of eggs, cream, and sliced Crottin de Chavignol, often presented with caramelized onions, herbs, or prosciutto, resulting in a rich, creamy interior perfect for a light lunch or elegant appetizer.

1.

Stracchino di Crescenza

Italy | **Soft** | **Cow, Buffalo**

Stracchino di crescenza is an Italian cheese typically made from cow's milk, although it can also be made with water buffalo's milk. This cheese has a creamy and buttery texture, making it often used as a spread. The flavors are mild, fruity, creamy, and sweet, making it a versatile addition to various dishes.

Historically, Stracchino di crescenza originated in the Po valley of Lombardy but is now also associated with the regions of Piedmont, Liguria, and Veneto. The name "stracchino" comes from the word "stracca," meaning tired, referring to the tired cows that move up and down the Alps. These cows produce rich milk, ideal for making this cheese.

For wine pairings, Stracchino di crescenza goes well with a fruity white wine such as Pinot Bianco or a light Prosecco. The wine's acidity and fruitiness balance the cheese's creamy and mild flavors, creating a pleasing overall tasting experience. This combination allows the subtle characteristics of the cheese to shine while providing a refreshing contrast with the wine's vibrant notes.

In Italian cuisine, Stracchino di crescenza is used in various ways. One popular dish is "Pizza Bianca," where the cheese is spread over the dough and topped with herbs and olive oil, creating a simple yet delicious pizza. Another favorite is "Pasta alla Crescenza," where the cheese is melted into a creamy sauce and mixed with freshly cooked pasta. Stracchino di crescenza is also used as a topping for warm polenta, adding a rich and creamy texture to the dish.

Additionally, the cheese is enjoyed with fresh fruit or cold cuts, making it a perfect addition to an antipasto platter. It pairs particularly well with grapes, and cured meats like prosciutto and salami, providing a balance of flavors and textures.

6. Pljevaljski Sir

Montenegro | **Soft** | **Cow**

Pljevaljski sir is a staple in many Montenegrin meals. This white cheese is traditionally made from raw cow's milk and is known for its strong flavor and creamy texture. Its unique aromas come from a maturation process that takes place in specially designed wooden barrels. The sliced cheese is salted, placed into the barrels, and then immersed in brine. It should mature for 15 days before it is ready for consumption.

Historically, Pljevaljski sir has been an integral part of Montenegrin culinary traditions. The method of using wooden barrels for maturation has been important, ensuring the cheese's distinctive characteristics. The annual event called Dani Pljevaljskog Sira celebrates this beloved cheese, where numerous producers from the Pljevalj region present their variations of Pljevaljski sir, highlighting its cultural significance.

For wine pairings, Pljevaljski sir pairs well with a medium-bodied red wine such as Vranac, a popular Montenegrin wine. The wine's fruitiness and slight acidity complement the cheese's strong flavor and creamy texture. Alternatively, a crisp white wine like Sauvignon Blanc can also be a good match, providing a refreshing contrast to the cheese's richness.

In Montenegrin cuisine, Pljevaljski sir is used in various dishes. One popular dish is "Gibanica," a savory pie made with layers of phyllo dough, eggs, and Pljevaljski sir, creating a rich and satisfying meal. Another favorite is "Pljevaljski sir with Njeguški pršut," where the cheese is served with Montenegrin prosciutto, olives, and fresh bread, making for a delicious appetizer or light meal. The cheese is also commonly used in salads, adding a creamy and tangy element to fresh vegetables and herbs.

Pljevaljski sir's strong flavor, traditional production methods, and versatility in cooking make it a cherished cheese in Montenegrin cuisine.

5. Burrata

Italy | **Soft** | **Cow**

Burrata, literally meaning "buttered," is an artisan cheese from the Puglia region of Southern Italy, particularly the provinces of Bari and Barletta-Andria-Trani. This cheese is handcrafted from cow's milk, rennet, and cream. It is believed that Lorenzo Bianchino Chieppa, a cheesemaker, created Burrata by forming a shell of stretched mozzarella strings and filling it with rich cream and smaller pieces of mozzarella.

The result is a cheese with a creamy interior and a rich flavor of fresh milk, quickly gaining popularity due to its unique texture and taste. Burrata should be eaten as fresh as possible, ideally within 24 hours of being made. It can be served alone, seasoned simply with salt, pepper, and a drizzle of extra virgin olive oil.

Historically, Burrata was developed as a way to use up the leftover curds from mozzarella production. The cheese was traditionally wrapped in asphodel leaves, which indicated its freshness as long as the leaves remained green. This method of production and packaging reflects the resourcefulness and culinary creativity of cheesemakers in Puglia.

For wine pairings, Burrata pairs well with light and crisp white wines such as Pinot Grigio or a dry Prosecco. The acidity and freshness of these wines complement the creamy richness of the cheese. A light pale rosé from Provence can also be an excellent pairing, providing a refreshing contrast to Burrata's texture.

In Italian cuisine, Burrata is used in various dishes to highlight its creamy qualities. One popular dish is "Caprese Salad with Burrata," where the cheese replaces traditional mozzarella, served with ripe tomatoes, fresh basil, and a drizzle of balsamic reduction. Another favorite is "Burrata Pizza," where the cheese is added to a hot pizza just before serving, allowing it to melt slightly over the top.

4. Queijo Serra da Estrela

Portugal | **Semi-Soft** | **Sheep**

Serra da Estrela is a semi-soft cheese made from the milk of the Bordaleira Serra da Estrela and Churra Mondegueira breeds of sheep. The milk is hand-milked, then heated, salted, and curdled using thistle extract. The curd is formed into cheeses and left to ripen in humid and cold conditions. The cheese has a creamy, semi-soft interior that is yellowish-white in color, with a flavor that is clean, sweet, and slightly sour. Serra da Estrela is Portugal's oldest and most traditional food product with international acclaim.

In the 13th century, the king of Portugal opened the first cheese market in Celorico da Beira, in the Serra da Estrela mountain range, where the cheese is still produced today. Historically, Serra da Estrela was so valued that it was present on some of the first ships to sail to the New World, showcasing its importance and long-standing heritage.

For wine pairings, Serra da Estrela pairs well with regional wines from the Dão region. A full-bodied red wine like Dão Tinto complements the cheese's rich, creamy texture and slightly sour flavor. The acidity and fruitiness of the wine balance the cheese's sweet and savory notes.

In Portuguese cuisine, Serra da Estrela is traditionally consumed as an appetizer or dessert. One popular way to enjoy it is simply spreading the creamy interior on broa, a local cornbread. Another favorite is "Queijo da Serra com Doce de Abóbora," where the cheese is served with a pumpkin jam, creating a delightful combination of sweet and savory flavors. Additionally, the cheese can be used in "Salada de Queijo da Serra," a salad featuring fresh greens, walnuts, and slices of Serra da Estrela cheese, dressed with olive oil and vinegar.

3. Mozzarella di Bufala

Italy | **Soft** | **Cow, Buffalo**

Mozzarella di Bufala is an Italian cheese made exclusively from 100% domestic water buffalo milk. It is produced in the regions of Campania, Lazio, Apulia, and Molise. Buffalo milk is known for being higher in calcium and protein while lower in cholesterol, making this mozzarella particularly prized and sought after. The cheese always comes packaged in brine and has a mild yet slightly sour taste, which pairs well with various Italian dishes.

Historically, Mozzarella di Bufala has been produced in Italy for centuries. The tradition dates back to the 12th century when water buffalo were introduced to Italy. The cheese quickly became a staple in the southern regions due to the high-quality milk produced by the buffalo. This cheese's production is now protected by the DOP (Denominazione di Origine Protetta) designation, ensuring that only mozzarella made from 100% buffalo milk and produced in specific regions can be labeled Mozzarella di Bufala Campana.

For wine pairings, Mozzarella di Bufala goes well with light, crisp white wines such as a Fiano di Avellino or a Falanghina. These wines complement the cheese's creamy texture and slightly sour flavor, enhancing the overall tasting experience. A young red wine like a Chianti can also be a good match, providing a nice balance.

In Italian cuisine, Mozzarella di Bufala is used in a variety of dishes. One of the most famous is the "Caprese Salad," where the cheese is sliced and paired with fresh tomatoes, basil, and a drizzle of extra virgin olive oil. Another popular dish is "Pizza Margherita," where slices of Mozzarella di Bufala are used as a topping, melting beautifully over the tomato sauce and basil. The cheese is also delicious in "Mozzarella in Carrozza," a traditional Italian fried sandwich where mozzarella is layered between slices of bread, dipped in egg, and fried until golden and crispy.

2

Graviera Naxou

Greece | **Hard** | **Sheep, Cow, Goat**

Graviera Naxou is a traditional Greek cheese that has been produced on the island of Naxos in the Cyclades for at least a century. Made from pasteurized cow milk or a mixture of sheep milk with up to 20% goat milk, this cheese boasts a thin rind and a light yellow, compact interior filled with small holes. Graviera Naxou is a hard table cheese with a refreshing taste and light aroma, reflecting the unique flora of the island that the local livestock graze on.

The cheese has a maximum moisture content of 38% and at least 40% fat content. The milk used in its production comes from breeds traditionally raised on Naxos, feeding on a diet of local plants and herbs that impart a distinctive flavor to their milk.

For wine pairings, Graviera Naxou pairs well with several Greek wines. A Xinomavro from Northern Greece is a great choice. Its complex flavors and firm tannins complement the cheese's richness without overshadowing it. Another excellent option is a Kalimera, a white wine from the Santorini region that, offers a crisp profile with notes of citrus and herbs that balance the cheese's creamy texture. Additionally, a Mandilaria, a red wine from Crete, pairs well due to its bold flavors and subtle spice, which harmonize with Graviera Naxou's distinctive taste.

In Greek cuisine, Graviera Naxou is quite versatile. It can be sliced and served as an appetizer, often drizzled with a bit of olive oil and accompanied by olives and bread. Another traditional use is grating the cheese over pasta dishes like "Makaronia Me Kima" (Greek-style spaghetti with meat sauce), adding a rich and flavorful topping. Additionally, Graviera Naxou is commonly used in "Moussaka," a classic Greek dish. In Moussaka, the cheese is layered between the spiced meat and eggplant, contributing a creamy texture and nutty flavor that enhances the overall dish. This traditional application showcases the cheese's ability to complement and elevate Greek comfort foods.

1. Parmigiano Reggiano

Italy | **Hard** | **Cow**

Considered the world's best cheese, Parmigiano Reggiano is made with raw, semi-skimmed milk from cows grazing on fresh grass and hay. It has a hard, gritty texture, and its flavors range from nutty to slightly piquant, depending on how long the cheese has matured.

The origins of Parmigiano Reggiano date back to the Middle Ages, when Benedictine and Cistercian monks reclaimed the Po Valley wetlands and began producing this highly prized cheese. The cheese originated and was primarily produced in the city-states of Parma and Reggio Emilia, hence the name Parmigiano Reggiano, which means "a cheese from Parma and Reggio Emilia." The name was established in the 19th century, with the order possibly due to alphabetical arrangement.

Today, Parmigiano Reggiano is produced in the provinces of Parma, Reggio Emilia, Modena, and Bologna in Emilia-Romagna, as well as in the Lombardian province of Mantua. It is available in several varieties: Mezzano (second selection, aged for 12-15 months), Parmigiano Reggiano (aged for 12-24 months or longer), and Parmigiano Reggiano Extra, which passes an additional quality assessment test after 18 months.

For wine pairings, Parmigiano Reggiano pairs well with full-bodied red wines such as Chianti or Barolo. These wines complement the cheese's complex flavors and slightly piquant taste.

In Italian cuisine, Parmigiano Reggiano is an essential ingredient in numerous classic dishes. It is ideal for grating over pasta, minestrone, and consommé, adding a rich depth of flavor. One popular dish is "Risotto alla Parmigiana," where the cheese is stirred into creamy risotto, creating a luxurious texture. Another classic is "Pasta al Parmigiano," a simple dish where freshly cooked pasta is tossed with butter and generous shavings of Parmigiano Reggiano.

Soft	Semi - Soft	Hard	Semi - Hard
29	19	24	28

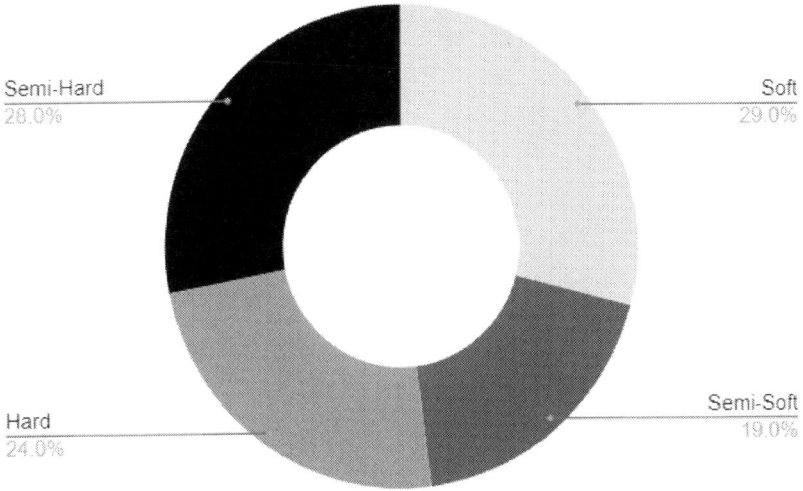

Semi-Hard
28.0%

Soft
29.0%

Hard
24.0%

Semi-Soft
19.0%

Goat	Cow	Buffalo	Sheep
29	61	5	41

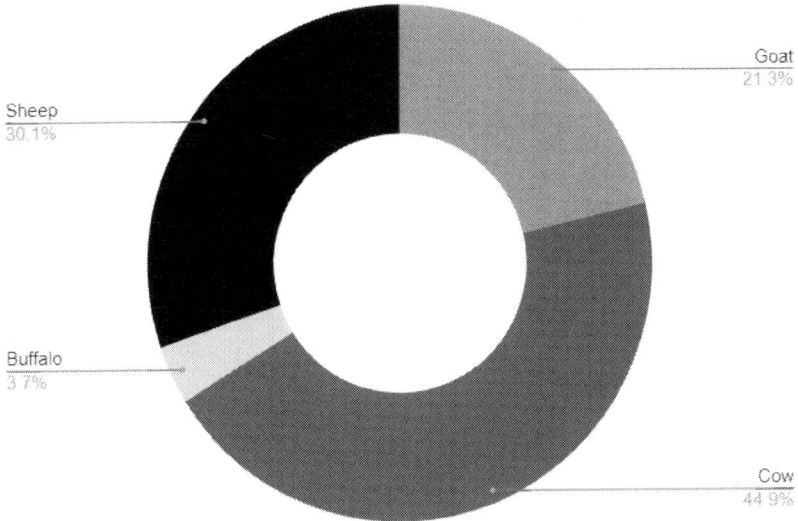

Sheep
30.1%

Goat
21.3%

Buffalo
3.7%

Cow
44.9%

Shares of top 100 cheeses by countries

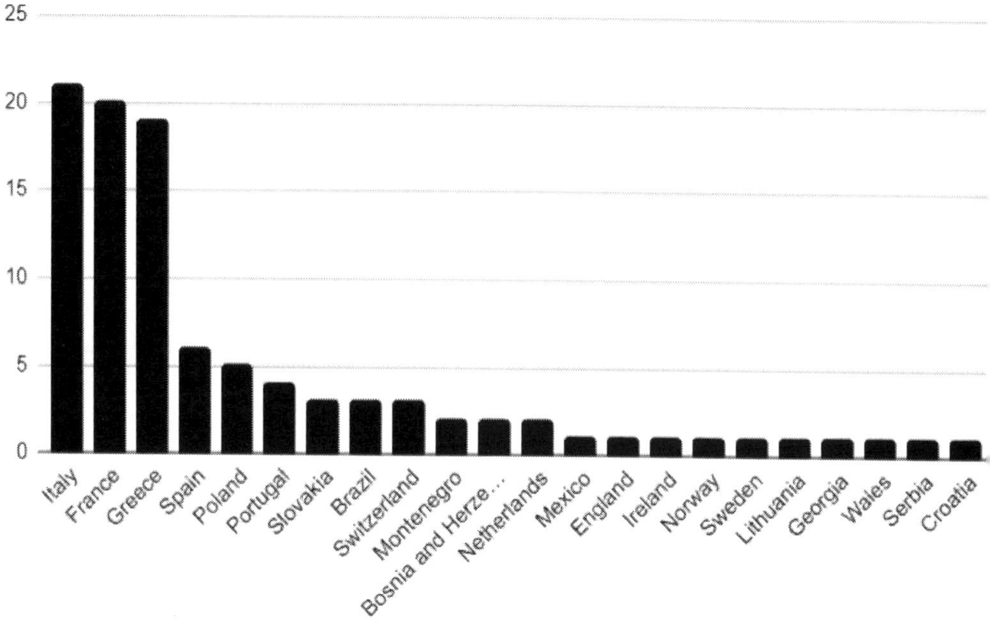
25
20
15
10
5
0
Italy
France
Greece
Spain
Poland
Portugal
Slovakia
Brazil
Switzerland
Montenegro
Bosnia and Herze...
Netherlands
Mexico
England
Ireland
Norway
Sweden
Lithuania
Georgia
Wales
Serbia
Croatia

World consumption of cheese by countries

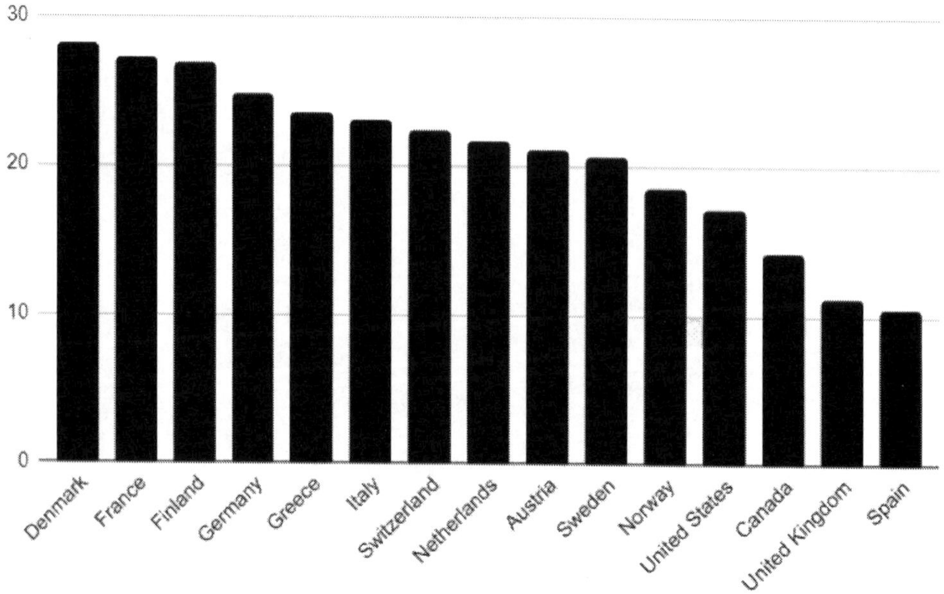
30
20
10
0
Denmark
France
Finland
Germany
Greece
Italy
Switzerland
Netherlands
Austria
Sweden
Norway
United States
Canada
United Kingdom
Spain

Ranking & Ratings

100. Prästost - 4.21

99. Fontina - 4.23

98. Dubliner - 4.24

97. Sbrinz - 4.24

96. Caña de Cabra - 4.26

95. Oscypek - 4.28

94. Tomme des Pyrénées - 4.28

93. Saint Agur - 4.29

92. Queijo Minas - 4.29

91. Kraftkar - 4.29

90. Tomme de Savoie - 4.29

89. Boerenkaas - 4.29

88. Feta - 4.29

87. Scamorza - 4.3

86. Bagoss - 4.3

85. Queijo de Coalho - 4.3

84. Slovenská Parenica - 4.3

83. Queijo de Cabra Transmontano - 4.3

82. Saint-Marcellin - 4.3

81. Selles-sur-Cher - 4.3

80. Caciocavallo Silano - 4.31

79. Liliputas - 4.31

78. Formaella Arachovas Parnassou - 4.31

77. Raclette de Savoie - 4.31

76. Gorgonzola dolce - 4.31

75. Morbier - 4.33

74. Époisses - 4.33

73. Paški sir - 4.33

72. Y Fenni - 4.33

71. Slovenský Oštiepok - 4.33

70. Pecorino Siciliano - 4.33

69. Stracciatella - 4.33

68. Cabécou - 4.33

67. Manchego curado - 4.34

66. Picón Bejes-Tresviso - 4.35

65. Kasseri - 4.35

64. Melichloro - 4.35

63. Myzithra - 4.36

62. Provola - 4.36

61. Ladotyri Mytilinis - 4.36

60. Brie de Melun - 4.37

59. Manchego Fresco - 4.37

58. Sfela - 4.38

57. Mastelo Cheese - 4.38

56. Queijo Serpa - 4.38

55. Sir iz mijeha - 4.38

54. Old Amsterdam - 4.38

53. Tête de Moine - 4.38

52. Metsovone - 4.38

51. Gruyère - 4.39

Ranking & Ratings

50. Sulguni - 4.39

49. Arseniko Naxou - 4.39

48. Taleggio - 4.39

47. Gorgonzola piccante - 4.39

46. Kefalotyri - 4.39

45. Livanjski sir - 4.39

44. Bryndza Podhalańska - 4.4

43. San Michali - 4.4

42. Queso Payoyo - 4.4

41. Burrata di Andria - 4.4

40. Gołka - 4.41

39. Njeguški Sir - 4.41

38. Manchego viejo - 4.41

37. Krasotyri - 4.41

36. Graviera Agrafon - 4.41

35. Beaufort - 4.42

34. Picodon - 4.43

33. Oaxaca Cheese - 4.43

32. Anthotyro - 4.43

31. Bundz - 4.43

30. Ovčí Salašnícky Údený Syr - 4.44

29. Redykołka - 4.44

28. Provolone del Monaco - 4.44

27. Miročki sir - 4.45

26. Kefalograviera - 4.45

25. West Country Cheddar - 4.46

24. Stracciata - 4.47

23. Délice de Bourgogne - 4.48

22. Canastra - 4.48

21. Comté - 4.49

20. Pecorino Toscano - 4.5

19. Queijo de Azeitão - 4.5

18. Pecorino Sardo - 4.5

17. Brillat-Savarin - 4.5

16. Kalathaki Limnou - 4.51

15. Pecorino Romano - 4.51

14. Grana Padano - 4.52

13. Mont d'Or - 4.52

12. Reblochon - 4.52

11. Graviera Kritis - 4.54

10. Saint-Félicien - 4.55

09. Saint-André - 4.55

08. Crottin de Chavignol - 4.56

07. Stracchino di Crescenza - 4.57

06. Pljevaljski Sir - 4.57

05. Burrata - 4.61

04. Queijo Serra da Estrela - 4.61

03. Mozzarella di Bufala - 4.62

02. Graviera Naxou - 4.67

01. Parmigiano Reggiano - 4.69

Printed in Great Britain
by Amazon

54462508R00059